Blues to BLISS

NGINA OTIENDE

For Tommy
My love and best friend

Contents

Introduction

"How is marriage?" A few months married, the question is as common as my morning cup of tea.

I know what folks want to hear. That marriage is fun and exhilarating, that I am swinging from the chandeliers in absolute glee twenty four hours a day. But while marriage is fun and exciting, it's not always fun, and certainly not always exciting.

So I tell people what I think they want to hear: "Oh marriage is awesome! It's fantastic!"

I leave the latter part for my mentors. The ones who know the real us, the ones who can tell when something is off, the ones who won't relent until we get this marriage thing straight.

That said, I would discover that even they couldn't "cure everything wrong" with my marriage. It took a long time - and moving thousands of miles away - to begin to understand the place of God and how to depend on Him for everything.

Almost every newlywed goes through what I call the "irritating questions" phase. That's when everyone wants to know everything about everything. Patting your flat belly and asking when the baby is coming. Giving you a once over and asking why you haven't gained any weight yet. Making up stories about your marriage because they saw you cry in a church service.

One of my chief irritations was the notion I would be giddy 24-7. Oh, I was happy, and my husband rocked. But marriage was much more than linking hands and keeping a smiley face. It involved successfully working out the hard details of a relationship without falling out of love.

Brides too have their days. It was not always sunshine. It was not always nice. And I reckoned that if someone wanted to hear the joys and good tidings of marriage, they should not flinch at the challenges and adjustments!

Signs of Life

New life brings with it a new set of challenges and mountains.

We don't take the first cries of a newborn baby as a sign there's something wrong with them. In fact, we are looking for that cry, and we celebrate it, because it signifies that everything is good with them.

The reality at this point is that two different people, from two different genders, with two different upbringings and life experiences have started living together as husband and wife. There are going to be some newborn cries and explosions! The noise and wriggling is not an indication that the marriage is doomed, but rather you are alive and there's a whole life ahead of you! The cries and squabbles of the early marriage years are a sign of life. Real life!

Marriage Requires Intentionality

If someone had told us on our wedding day that marriage would one day demand of us more than we could give, we'd have laughed them off.

That's because no one gets married to be miserable, or to make their spouse miserable. We all want happiness, joy and fulfillment, the kind that comes from spending the rest of our lives with the one we love.

However, we often don't realize that the kind of fulfillment we are looking for in marriage does not come automatically. Rather it's a result of consistent effort, commitment and a wholehearted pursuit of God.

Author and personal-development expert, the late Jim Rohn said, "The problem with drifting is that you cannot drift your way to the top of a mountain."

You can't achieve great things by merely wishing them into being! You have to get on some climbing boots and get to work.

As newlyweds and early weds, "work" is the last thing on our minds. We are dripping with "love hormones" and reckon feelings of love will coast us through every challenge and smoothen all rough patches. In other words, we think we won't have to work hard at marriage at all because... who does that? Love is enough!

But then at about Day 2 of marriage, he's no longer as attentive as he was. He's distracted and tardy. And he doesn't like to help around the house. In fact you have to ask for help when you need it! Gasp! You can't imagine not repeatedly asking (read *nagging*) him to change. And it's mighty hard to submit when you are so riled up.

The months roll by and things don't seem to improve. It gets harder to respond in the bedroom, and shutting down feels like the only response. Everyone around you continues to think that marriage is all fun and you keep wondering what planet they are from.

Clearly love, or the *feeling* of love, does not cure everything.

Did you miss something along the way? You begin to question yourself as you survey your struggles and difficulties. Is this what marriage is all about? Was it hoax? The delirious courtship, the happy wedding day, did it all lead to frustrations, anxiety, fear, miscommunication, conflict and downright hardheadedness?

Often, this is where we get stuck as newlyweds, hanging between the dreams and expectations we had before marriage and the stark reality of married life. We find ourselves wondering if the early marriage adjustments and challenges, the honeymoon blues, are an indication of absolute marriage breakdown.

I found myself there, and many young couples have been in these same shoes. They've imagined that being presented with a test means they have failed. And that can be a real doozy, because you can't make things better in marriage by digging yourself into a hole of hopelessness and despair. To move forward, you must face your reality head-on, dust off your pre-marital counseling notes, hold on to the hand of Jesus and get to work.

Every couple checks in at the marital reality stop - the disappointments and challenges common in the early years of marriage. *You are not alone.* Many couples have been there. But they chose not to *stay* there. Unless the early challenges are addressed, they grow and become older marriage blues; deep seated challenges and pains that clog the highway to your wedded bliss.

In this book, I want to cheer you through the kinks and challenges of the early marriage years. I want to explain the yelps and discomforts and help you understand that you can navigate, overcome and come out stronger.

You don't have to stay stuck in frustrations, fear and defeat. You don't have to throw things around to get your husband's attention. God can and will use you to change the dynamics of your relationship, but first, you have to align yourself to His will and begin to do life a different way. His way includes a lot of personal growth and a whole lot of love and grace showered on your man. And yourself.

What I mean by "Happily-ever-after"

When I talk about creating a happily-ever-after, I am not talking about attaining a fairytale state of happiness in marriage. I am not a fan of seeking "happiness" as the world understands it. I believe in joy, that exuberant, deep feeling of peace, gladness and contentment that is not dependant on our physical circumstance but bubbles from within as a result of knowing whose we are.

So wherever you see me talking about a happily ever after, I am talking about that state of marriage where both of you are constantly growing, reaching towards what God has called you to and joyfully so. Like Paul, you and your husband might be able to say,

"Not that I have already attained, or am already perfected; but I press on, that I may lay hold of that for which Christ Jesus has also laid hold of me."

A Caveat - This Is For Wives!

I am writing primarily to wives, and specifically, those who feel like marriage is a lot more difficult than they bargained for, who feel their husbands could do with a little (or a whole lot of) changing. I am suspecting that's most wives, but if that's not you, well, I still welcome you to walk the pages with us.

While I am writing to wives and encouraging them to take responsibility for their marriage, I am not suggesting they are solely responsible for the success of marriage. Husbands are responsible too. They have a role to play. After all, you can't create a happily-ever-after all by yourself!

Nonetheless, in my own marriage, I have discovered that the only person I am responsible for, the only person I can change is me. Not Tommy.

My heart in this book is not to put the burden of "success" on you as a wife, but to show you *your* part in laying a strong foundation for your marriage. It's about helping you to become better as a person, and as a result, the Lord may use you to change your marriage. It takes two to tango or tangle, but make no mistake, one person can determine the health and success of a relationship. They can be the joint on which the whole marriage begins to pivot.

And that person, as far as this book is concerned, is you. I don't want to sound like a broken record, but I need you to understand my heart so that you don't take offense down the pages when I speak some tough-love. It's not that your husband does not have a role play. But that would be another book, preferably written by my husband! This book is for wives who want to know how to make their marriages better, their role in moving their marriage from blues-land to bliss-land.

Some of the things I am about to take you through are challenging to put to practice. I struggled when God began to prod me in the direction of intentionality because all I desired was for Him to prod my husband. I believed I was alright! Or at least better than my man. I've had to learn and apply these things first, and I am still learning.

I feel that if wives could concentrate on getting better as individuals, if we could work on removing bitterness and discouragement from our hearts, we would see big improvements in our marriages. You don't need another book to tell you how wrong your husband is! You need someone to teach you how to respond better. You need someone to encourage you to pursue God when it's rough, someone to encourage you to get on your knees and seek the Lord and pray for your marriage. You don't need another gossipy girlfriend or someone to tell you how right and justified you are in doing whatever you wish.

I am not saying your husband is right, I am not even insinuating you are the problem in your marriage. All I am saying is that God can use you to change the direction of your marriage, no matter where you are. You might not get your desired results today or tomorrow. Your answers might not come packaged exactly the way you want. But God will break through for you, if you stand your ground and refuse to quit. God can do that impossible thing but first you must allow Him to work in you.

Galatians 6:4-5 NLT says, "Pay careful attention to your own work, for then you will get the satisfaction of a job well done, and you won't need to compare yourself to anyone else. For we are each responsible for our own conduct."

I pray that as we walk down the pages together, God will begin to stir a hunger and thirst for a greater thing in your marriage. I pray that you will be thoroughly challenged in your thoughts, faith and habits.

I truly believe that if God can reach our hearts, He can reach our situations. Things might look tough and your marriage situation might look hopeless, but God is an expert at the hopeless and impossible. As you read along, be encouraged that it doesn't take two for marriage to begin to turn around. Sometimes, it just takes one. And that one can be you.

Walk Down Memory Lane

Our Premarital Days

"Y ou will know that I am a prophet when you get married!" These are oft repeated words of Johnny Umukoro, our Pastor and pre-marital counselor.

Sheepish grins and long laughter follow his wisecrack on marriage realities. The laughter calms our eager, but otherwise blissfully naïve minds.

Tommy and I had the longest (boy, doesn't courtship last forever!), intensive, but most rewarding pre-marital counseling season.

Let me start by sharing a little bit about us.

We first saw each other at a leadership class that we both facilitated at our local church. We managed to go through a whole semester without ever noticing one another. Then one afternoon, I walked into the Sanctuary and noticed, for the first time, a fine, lean man in a crisp suit collecting bibles and books from the pews.

My first thought? My, my. That's a fine dude... I am sure he wouldn't have eyes for me! (Don't you laugh at me because I know you too have had foolish thoughts that need to see the side of a kerb!)

Eventually, Tommy and I got talking. We hang out during class breaks and I was fascinated by his rich, deep voice, wide shoulders and sexy walk (not that I could have said the latter back then!) Tommy on the other hand was becoming more fascinated with my brilliant mind, red streaks in my hair and shiny jewelry on my tooth.

We became fast friends. After a while, we began hanging out, outside the leadership class settings with another friend. You know, accountability and all. Within no time we were exchanging tones of emails, and not wanting to drag my heart through inane feelings, I asked, in the nicest way possible, what our friendship was all about, if it had an agenda.

Tommy's response was that *my* Daddy had said no to anything more than a friendship. I should have been glad that at least the man prays and hears from God, and I was, to a degree. But I was also crushed because I really liked him.

After this "clarification," we kept a distant friendship for about two years, and then things started cooking again. But this time I had just lost my dad and my heart was a mess and I did not know if I was feeling and hearing my own things. So I went before God, praying and fasting. If you are reading this and you are single and all confused about a guy, you might want to try that.

Anyway, God would work out the situation and we eventually got peace and go-ahead from God and our pastors. Not to go ahead and get married, but to explore if we were meant to be together.

It turned out that we were.

That's how we found ourselves seated every Tuesday morning for several months with Pastor Johnny as we prepared for marriage. Our premarital sessions were intense! So much so that we sometimes wondered if our pastors were trying to bring us together or break us apart!

Later in marriage we began to understand what the Pastors were doing; preparing us for real marriage! They were trying to drill into our giddy hearts the sacredness and depth of marriage, and teach us what it takes to make a marriage work. We figured that the impartation received during courtship and premarital counseling had to be heavy, enough to make you want to despair and break up altogether! If it wasn't heavy, then you missed crucial parts in the pre-marriage journey.

Just like salvation, it is when we come to the end of ourselves that God can truly take over and help us. Any true relationship must head south aka "die" before it can live. Serious and deep challenges, if they do not make us bail out, will usually make us run to God for answers. They grow us, help us give up our little "rights" and self-righteous ways. It is when we end that God comes alive in our own hearts and relationships.

After the wedding, one of the things that struck us most about marriage was the permanence of it. "Until death do us part" is a very long time indeed! Which is why, at a light bulb moment, we stood amazed at the many people, waddling and sashaying down the aisle to get married "because they fell in love!"

Considering that marriage is the biggest cure for the "in-love" syndrome (the day you get married is the day you get cured, how about that), it's a frightening thought that we'd marry for love alone.

Lest you close this book in despair, it's great to be in love! But the initial love we have when we get married hasn't been tested. That fuzzy, romantic love, which my husband likes to call "bait," is the delicious carrot, which draws us to the next level: the real deal. Without the "carrot," we wouldn't want the main dish, marriage, where the real details of love exist.

It is in marriage where we learn that the real spelling for the word love is *Commitment*. The throngs of people who sign up for the love class but fail in that spelling test is astounding. That romantic feeling of love must grow and mature into something even greater if we are to have lasting wedded bliss.

Start of Honeymoon Blues

Two days after our wedding, we took a cab ride from our brief honeymoon stay and headed home to start life together. We were as happy and giddy as any newlyweds can be. And tired.

Utterly completely exhausted.

We arrived at our doorstep and Tommy stopped me. He wanted to carry me across the threshold. He cracked open the door, but instead of sweeping me into his arms, quickly excused himself and took off in the direction of the kitchen. (Later, I would discover a very moldy pot sitting at our kitchen balcony.)

His brief exit gave me an opportunity to survey the living room.

It was a mess. Electronics, gift boxes in all shapes, sizes and colors, unwrapped gifts, cards, a bed, all littered the living area. Our friends had dumped a truckload of wedding gifts and items on our living room floor. There was barely room to put two feet on.

"*Who in the world will clean up this mess!*" I wailed in silent horror as Tommy carried me across the threshold.

I guess that first day should have been a heads-up on what it takes to build a real marriage. I should have realized that temporary honeymoon was easy to pull off, but lasting marital bliss was not a walk in the park.

Now, it wasn't *wrong* to expect a neat house. And it's not wrong to expect a smooth start to marriage. There's nothing wrong with good expectation. In fact, God wants us to have great expectations! (Hebrews 11:1) But sometimes, our good expectations will not be met and it's what we do at that point on that matters.

We can sit back and wish for a healthy relationship. Wish that someone would scrub the pan in the balcony, vacuum the carpets and put the items in their place. We can wish for better communication and mind blowing sex, wish that we could break him out of his man cave and feel like submitting.

We can *wish* but unless we *do* something, we'll be steeped in honeymoon blues year in, year out.

If you are like me or most brides in the early years, you might not like the gospel of hard work. We adore the nice, yummy marriage but dislike all the effort it takes to get there. We'd rather cruise down the river on a bamboo boat, popping coconuts and singing happy songs all day long without having to catch us some fish.

But all good things require effort. Happiness and joy and fulfillment isn't handed to us on a silver platter. We need to get rid of this idea that if we are meant to be happy in marriage, happiness will automatically find us. We need to put on our big girl pants - or dresses - and realize that intentional work is what bridges the gap between the dreams in our heads and the reality of married life.

Marriage as an institution has never been the problem. The problem is always the two human beings involved. Their selfishness, ego, pride, *sin*. Author Judith Viorst has said, "One advantage of marriage is that, when you fall out of love with him or he falls out of love with you, it keeps you together until you fall in again."

Marriage is meant to keep people together, not just when things are good, but *particularly* when they are not. That's why you take marriage vows - not wishes. It's a covenant that binds you together regardless of your circumstances.

While "statistics" indicate that 33 to 50 percent of today's marriages end in divorce, no one said your marriage is supposed to be part of that statistic. (And, by the way, that statistic is not true for true believers) [1]

I'm saying that to say that when challenges swing by your newlywed gates, it's not the time to get discouraged and depressed. It's not the time to work longer hours, throw tantrums, withdraw, sulk, blame, refuse to take responsibility for the happiness and growth of the marriage. It's time to roll up your sleeves and get to work.

Being a last born child in a family of nine kids, one of my biggest shockers of marriage was this growing up part. It hit me right between the eyes! I couldn't believe just how grown up I was supposed to be. For most of my life, I had drifted by and escaped doing work I didn't like. Coming from a large family, someone else would inadvertently pick up the slack. My older sister washed clothes when I got myself busy with other things and "forgot" to wash them. I was - to my glee - the "worst cook" in the family and I rarely had cooking duties.

I expected to breeze through marriage pretty much the same way. I thought that whenever I faced something I didn't like - housework, dying to self, loving selflessly etc. I could just slack off and someone else, namely my husband, would pick up the slack and make everything good.

But I was in for a shocker.

It's Okay to Feel Lost

Before we move on, let me reiterate something.

It's okay to feel lost in the early days of marriage.

Oh, how I would have loved to hear those reassuring words, over and over again, those early days.

While my husband and I had the most amazing mentors, they also happened to be way ahead in years - over fifteen years of marriage tucked under their individual belts.

We kept measuring our progress and growth against theirs. And lost every single time.

Hear this from me, fellow wife (and husband reading through this). Every married person has moments when their dreams and hopes feel completely out of touch with reality.

I remember our mentor telling us that premarital counseling was a lot like teaching people how to swim while seated in a class. Reality would apply once they dove into the waters and began to exercise what they had learned in class. In this sense, marriage will always stretch us in ways we didn't even think existed before we hit the swimming pool of marriage.

The Challenges are for Good

One of the things I struggled with in those early days was the presence of conflict in our marriage. I looked at other young marriages and they looked perfect. A friend of mine, who I was trying to look up to, even mentioned that they did not have conflict in their marriage (though later, I suspected she and I had a different understanding of the word conflict). So after marriage I felt like we were crazy because "everyone else" was having a breeze while we had gazillion issues to overcome.

Of course, I'd learn that no one was having a breeze. Every couple has issues to iron out. If they don't, they are likely not being very honest with themselves! I couldn't tell that others were imperfect too, because I was looking from the outside.

The problem with looking from the outside is that you tend to compare yourself. As a result, you feel ashamed and discouraged about your struggles because you have built up this unrealistic picture in your mind of how a perfect marriage looks like. But this reality doesn't exist and so you end up working hard to create something that doesn't exist.

As we begin to look into specific "honeymoon blues," you will realize that anyone can pull their marriage off (or stop its advance towards) the edge of a cliff. *It's a matter of willingness and tenacity.* All marriages are salvageable as long as the people - or one person - involved are willing to put in the effort and work required to turn it around.

In the following chapters, we'll be looking at specific areas where couples need to pay special attention to in order to establish their marriage on a stronger foundation; the foundation of grace and intentional love.

Honeymoon blues, those moments when our hopes and dreams for marriage feel like they've taken flight, present great opportunities for growth.

In looking back, I am so thankful for all our early marriage struggles and challenges. Obviously I am still very young in marriage (we are six and a half years married by the time of writing this book) and there's so much more to learn. But in our short years, I can see how our bumps and blues have made us stronger.

Cultivating intimacy with God as the foundation for lasting bliss

"We can never have extraordinary relationships with our spouses when we are settling for an ordinary relationship with God."

Justin and Trisha Davis

Marriage is a gift from God. He wants you to enjoy a supernatural marriage, initial blues and bumps notwithstanding.

Marriage is supernatural because God's best does not have natural or average or mediocre attached to it. God is not *normal* and neither are His gifts, including the gift of marriage.

It therefore follows that for us to enjoy everything God has prepared for us in marriage, we must go deeper in Him.

In 1 Corinthians 2:9-10, we read "...as it is written: "Eye has not seen, nor ear heard, nor have entered into the heart of man, the things which God has prepared for those who love Him." But God has revealed them to us through His Spirit. For the Spirit searches all things, yes, the deep things of God.""

There are things that God wants to reveal to you and give you in your marriage that don't originate with human action or human thought. There is a depth that God wants to take you to that is beyond words in a book. I cannot reach that depth for you. Neither can your pastor, mentor or Bible study group. Only the Spirit of God can submerge you in its wonder.

While we all struggle from time to time, God does not want you to be defined by your struggle or pain. Instead, He wants you to push past the blues as you get deeper in Him and *catch* his heart, because wedded bliss lies on the other side of the storm.

There is no shortcut to a glorious marriage. If you want a happy, God-centered marriage, you must be centered in Christ. To have an extraordinary marriage, you must have an intimate connection with the extraordinary God. A connection that is not lukewarm or lackluster, but blazing, alive and real. You must be getting into His Word and learning for yourself what it means to be a child of the Most High God, a daughter of the King and a wife to His son (that's your husband).

Many of us come into marriage thinking that our husbands will satisfy us. In fact, some of us chose a husband over God. We gave up on God's timing, took matters into our own hands and found a man for ourselves. If you are in this position, there is no condemnation. *But I want you to know that God is waiting for you to come back home.* You may have walked out on Him but He did not walk out in you. He wants you to come back to relationship with Him because without Him, you can do nothing (John 15:5).

Your husband does not have the answers you seek. God is the only One that can fully satisfy and fill the holes in your heart.

You must be thirsty and passionate for God in a way you've never been before. You must build a foundation of intimacy with God, because He wants us to experience a supernatural love, a depth and intimacy that is founded on His supernatural abilities, not on mere human efforts and abilities.

What is Intimacy?

Having the revelation about God and what He desires for marriage is not enough. We must *invest* in intimacy with Him, turning to Him for answers, day by day, moment by moment. Many of us live by the old adage, "If everything else fails, try prayer!" But God must not be a last resort in your life or marriage!

The dictionary defines intimacy as "a close, familiar, and usually affectionate or loving personal relationship with another person."

Typically, when husbands hear the word "intimacy," they think about sex! Wives, on the other hand, think about friendship, touching, kissing, talking, hugging, cuddling. It's a good thing they don't think the same, because together, a husband and wife make a complete whole! Intimacy in marriage is not just about sex. Neither is it all about talking or cuddling.

Intimacy in marriage involves staying connected mentally, emotionally, socially, financially, spiritually, physically, and sexually. It doesn't have to be a perfect connection, but there must be a consistent effort to stay connected.

In the same way, being intimate with God will require deliberate and consistent effort from *all* of you, not some part of you and certainly not some of the time.

Let me share a caveat here; people who are not intimate with God can have "good" marriages. They're good in the sense that they have grasped some principles and put them to work, reaping some type of happiness. But they still lack the life that comes from connecting to and having a thriving relationship with the author of marriage. They don't have the power and revelation to do marriage God's way because they are not intimate with God!

And so in the end and as long as your spiritual life is limping (or non-existent), your marriage will limp on the inside, even when it looks normal on the outside.

As we discussed earlier, God does not want His children to have good or average marriages. He wants our marriages to rock! He wants our marriages to preach the gospel of love without ever having to say a word. That can only happen when we are completely in tune with Him.

Intimacy Is A Journey

Think about the process that led to your own wedding day. The butterflies of the early days, the excitement of friendship, the stretch of courtship, the crescendo of engagement and marriage - the journey to wifehood was not without effort.

Intimacy with God is a similar journey. It starts with the realization that without having an intimate relationship with the author of marriage, you lack the power to carry out His mandate in marriage. Once you have this understanding, it follows that you will seek His active and complete involvement in your life and marriage.

Your husband didn't just fall into your life with an all-access pass. You first gave him permission. God is a gentleman and will not impose Himself on us. We must give him access. Now, it's entirely possible to accept Jesus into your heart and not allow Him into all areas of your life.

My pastor says the way you know that Jesus is Lord over your life is when He has veto-power. When Christ gives you instructions and you obey, when you allow Him to influence your behavior, form your character, direct your paths - *then* you know Jesus is leading your life.

If you are constantly ignoring His voice, debating His clear instructions and shrugging off His still small voice, then He's probably not the Lord of your life. You are.

Losing your life in Christ is the first step towards building intimacy with God and ultimately creating a great marriage.

Growing in Intimacy with God

For those of you who are mature in your walk with Christ, the basics of growing with God may seem familiar or "old," but we can all do with a reminder. For those who are just starting your relationship with Christ, be encouraged that taking these deliberate efforts to grow intimacy with God makes a difference in our lives and marriages.

Here are ways to grow and tend your relationship with God and have it impact your marriage:

1. Spend time with God
Talking with my husband is one of my favorite things. In fact, you'll find me trying to carry on conversations over the distance. He'll be in the living room and I'll be in the bedroom and I'll be going on as if he were sitting right next to me. (If you are a husband reading this book, now you know your wife is not the only crazy one!)

But there's always a hitch with our "long distance conversations." He misses parts of my talk. I strain to hear his booming voice as it bounces across walls. I get frustrated when he doesn't respond to something I said (because he didn't hear it!).

It's the same way when talking to God. "Long distance" relationship does not work! You need to be close to Him, tenderly cultivating your relationship, taking time to listen to what He's saying, creating the right atmosphere for good communication. It's not that God can't hear you (remember He's omnipresent) but that *you* can't hear Him when you wander away.

We're exhorted in Matthew 6:6: "But you, when you pray, go into your room, and when you have shut your door, pray to your Father who is in the secret place; and your Father who sees in secret will reward you openly"

You can't be off doing your own thing, multitasking and hoping to have fruitful conversation with God. Slow down, shut yourself in a room, curve out seasons of prayer and worship and lean close to God.

In his letter to Timothy, a young pastor in Ephesus, Paul, the older, more experienced apostle says,

"Work hard so you can present yourself to God and receive his approval. Be a good worker, one who does not need to be ashamed and who correctly explains the word of truth." 2 Timothy 2:15 NLT

Notice the beginning words "work hard." Timothy was a young Pastor charged with the heavy responsibility of taking care of the church in the city of Ephesus. While you and I might not be called to pastor a church, we are called to be witness of God's glorious salvation to others (Acts 1:8). At any given time we are shining our light and being an example to those around us, our families, colleagues at work, neighbors.

So work hard. Don't rely on your pastor to do what you need to be doing yourself. Do your own praying and read your own bible. Don't limit your relationship with God to a small segment in the morning or evening. Allow Him into the rest of your day. Let your thoughts be turned towards Him as you drive to work or take a bus. Talk to Him as you do your grocery shopping. Turn your heart towards Him and ask for wisdom when you'd rather spout off at your husband. God wants to commune with us, not in spurts or special moments only, but every moment of our life. He wants us to have a real, natural relationship.

2. Obey what He tells you to do

Do you have someone in your life who never seems to agree with you? Think about your relationship with that person. You feel like you are constantly on the battlefield. If you say anything that really matters, you know he or she will have the opposite opinion. As soon as an idea pops into your head, your blood pressure starts to rise as you imagine the response you will get.

You can't be intimate with someone you don't agree with on a consistent basis.

The same goes for intimacy with God. Being in agreement with God means that you agree with what God says, not the other way round.

I had a yo-yo relationship with God in my early years as a Christian. I gave my life to the Lord as a teenager, but it wasn't until I was much older that we attained "flow." Throughout my teenage years, God would talk to me and convict me about the kind of music I was listening to, the books I was reading, the type of friends I was keeping. I felt the conviction but I loved my music and novels and friends too much to give them up. So for the first seven years of my salvation, God and I were not particularly intimate. I was running from his conviction. Nonetheless, God never left me, He actually kept me on a type of leash (I could only do so much). But our relationship was handicapped by my disobedience.

Like me, most of us struggle with the idea of yielding control and submitting to authority. We balk at giving up control, even when it's for our own good. As a society, we are independent and want to control our lives and future - hence the attraction of the "American dream." People want to be safe and secure, but security does not come from holding your life in your own hands but from yielding your life to your Creator and allowing Him to lead your life.

God did not create us to control life but to submit to Him and in Him find real freedom and life. He knew you before He wove you in your mother's womb. He assigned you destiny before you were born. Would God be so involved before your very existence, and then leave you to fend for yourself once you were born? No. God has a good plan for your life.

The Bible says in Romans 8: 29 – 30 NLT

"For God knew his people in advance, and he chose them to become like his Son, so that his Son would be the firstborn among many brothers and sisters. And having chosen them, he called them to come to him. And having called them, he gave them right standing with himself. And having given them right standing, he gave them his glory."

The Creator of heaven and earth knows not just your physical DNA but your spiritual and eternal DNA. You can afford to lean close to Him and obey what He says because He is trustworthy (Psalms 19:7).

3. Cultivate passion
In his book, "When Sinners Say I Do," Dave Harvey defines zeal thus:

"Zeal is a desire on steroids. An average football fan sits in the stands and cheers, but a zealous one will sit shirtless in sub-freezing weather with his body painted in team colors. Zeal is people who get up at 5am on Black Friday to stand in the dark to score a bargain. Zeal is a deep desire that defines how we live and reveals what we love..."[1]
If you were to sit next to me in a church service, you'd see me dancing and clapping. I know not everybody's like that (although it'd be nice to have some company!). But as you grow your intimacy with the Lord, it's important to allow some of that life within you to ooze out! Let it affect your outside – allow it to define your worship, your life, what you treasure.

God won't force zeal or passion on us. In any case, we shout and jump at football games out of our own will, without anybody having to tell us to! We are just passionate and it oozes out and affects the way we act. While God does convict and woo our hearts, ultimately, the resounding "yes!" has to come from us.

And not just once, but continuously.

On your wedding day, you said, "I love you and want to spend the rest of my life with you." Hopefully, that wasn't the only time you said those words. You continue to affirm them throughout marriage, in your thoughts and deeds and words. In the same way and through the challenges, doubts, fears, joys, successes of life, you have to continue saying yes to God and fanning the passion.

Obviously, we all have moments where we're tempted to slacken. We all know those days when you know you need to spend time with God, but instead, you wander off into the living room and end up vegging out in front of the TV. Or those days you've found yourself fighting with your husband over yet another silly thing instead of shutting up, listening and exploring your part in his wound. The point is that there'll be moments when you'll have to work hard to do the right thing. Press through those moments and do the right thing anyway.

One last thing; some people believe that living for the Lord is boring. In fact, they feel like God is boring!

Think with me for a moment: How can the One who created the galaxies and oceans and stars, curved mountains and hillsides and forests, spoke things into being, be dull or lifeless? How can the God who created man to mind-blowing detail and complexities be passionless? How can the God who created you in His own image not create in you a thirst and passion for life and relationship?

I put it to you that God is not dull!

Rekindle your passion and thirst for God! You have the capacity. If you can cheer that loud for your favorite football team, then you have capacity to pursue God just as loudly!

4. Allow intimacy with God to breed honesty with yourself

I find that God is like a mirror. You know how mirrors don't lie, right? Unless you are in one those departmental stores! Typically, a clean mirror reflects back your true form. You can cry and deny it all you want, but the mirror does not change its mind. Therefore, an honest (or sane) person does not pick a fight with the mirror, but rather understands where to process reality - within, not without.

When I was a single girl, I had a very high opinion of myself. To my shame, I wondered how married couples could have conflicts and still claim to love God. I could think like that because I was standing very far from the marriage mirror. When Tommy came into my life, he began to expose weaknesses, issues and sins I didn't even know existed. Eventually I'd begin to see God as *the* mirror, using my marriage to show me areas I needed to grow in. He had placed Tommy and I into each other's life so we could sharpen each other and become more like Him.

Like a trusted mirror, God will reveal the shadows and places that need growth as we grow closer to him. He reveals not only our flaws and sins (which we can see with our natural eyes), but also reflects who we are in Him - redeemed, whole, and complete. He doesn't leave you staring at your struggling marriage. He opens your eyes so He can help you overcome, and so you can understand how much you need Him.

Some of our biggest marital problems stem from a lack of honesty with God and with ourselves. We fight with truth-tellers instead of accepting that they are just but vessels. Can you remember the last time you had a big blow-up with your husband? If you really think about it, the reason it became a big thing was because one (or both) of you was unwilling to be honest with yourself. Imagine what a difference, *"I am sorry, I should have been more sensitive and not said what I said, will you please forgive me?"* would have made. Instead, the moment *"Why can't you take some honest opinion?"* ran out of your mouth, it became a bumpy race up ego mountain.

Matthew 7:3 NIV says "Why do you look at the speck of sawdust in your brother's eye and pay no attention to the plank in your own eye?"

Don't you just love how God shows you the three fingers pointing back at you when you wag a finger at your husband? Getting closer to God will give you a clear vision. You will begin to see your role in creating a happily-ever-after, not just hoping for it!

5. Be poured out (because selfishness will kill intimacy)
Have you ever walked into a roomful of kids and immediately picked out the problem child?

He's walking around the room, holding onto a bunch of toys, trying to grab other toys from other kids and screaming his lungs out when they refuse to hand them over? Of course you think, "I'd hate to be that kid's parent," (even when you are!).

But we do that all the time in our marriages, don't we? We try to make the relationship all about ourselves - our feelings, our opinions, our remote control, our preference, our 'rights.' We throw a big tantrum when our spouse refuses to hand over the toys.

Selfishness is one of the biggest reasons young couples walk out on each other. By walk out, I mean "check out" of the relationship - disconnect from their spouse mentally, emotionally and sexually.

Matthew 26 tells us about a woman named Mary Magdalene who anointed Jesus with oil.

"And when Jesus was in Bethany at the house of Simon the leper, a woman came to Him having an alabaster flask of very costly fragrant oil, and she poured it on His head as He sat at the table."

The jar was beautiful, the oil was expensive. And it was poured out, not sparsely or sparingly. *Lavishly poured out.* While the disciples fussed about her action, Jesus was pleased and went on to say that wherever the gospel would be preached, Mary's story would be told as a memorial to her!

Intimacy with the Lord will always require a pouring out of ourselves. You can't hold back and keep the most precious part of your life from Him, yet desire to be intimate with Him.

Philippians 2:6 tells us that Jesus did not hold on to His deity but became humble and broken for our sakes. He did it so He could bring us back to relationship with the Father. In asking us to be prefer another before ourselves, God is not asking us to do something He hasn't already done.

The Intimacy Thief

Even as you pursue intimacy with God, there's an enemy who doesn't want you to deepen your relationship with God. He knows that if you lock your eyes and soul on Jesus, he stands to lose the battle for your marriage. He knows that if he can have your attention, he can have your marriage.

Listen to his words to Eve, the first wife on earth, in Genesis 3:1 *"Has God indeed said, 'You shall not eat of every tree of the garden?"*

Notice those sly words. He wasn't going at Eve with big blazing guns. He knew that if he was too blatant or obvious, she would sniff him out. So he tried to get her to question the truth she knew.

In my short years of marriage and from talking with other wives, I've discovered the enemy doesn't always like to soil his hands trying to hang our marriages. Often, he will hand us a rope and watch as we finish the job. The moment we listen to his lies, we start questioning God's truth and he watches gleefully as we tumble and fall.

I don't know what kind of a day Eve was having, but I do know that as women, we are most vulnerable when we are going through something.

Waiting on a promise. Facing a big challenge and God feels far away. Unable to wrap our minds around a trial. Or maybe just idle and curious.

Any time the enemy has a chance, he will try to get us to question the goodness and plans of God for our marriage. He will play on our fears, try to work through our selfishness, even ignorance. He will twist the truth and present it as a "higher" alternative.

As a newlywed, the devil did this very number on me. He managed to convince me that it was hypocritical to try and connect with God when we had unresolved issues with my husband.

As a single, I'd heard that after marriage God would either see *both* of us or *none* of us. Once I got married, I believed that unless it was sunny and fuzzy in Otiende-land, God could not step through our doors. Unfortunately, it wasn't always warm and fuzzy. We were newlyweds, learning the ropes of marriage. We had issues from here to heaven; from small irritations to full blown conflicts.

In those stormy seasons, I believed that God's ears were shut to our prayers. These were not obvious thoughts, and it wasn't until God began to reveal the source of my fear and despair that I began to see the dark trail.

As God exposed the lies I had believed, He reminded me that He was not a seasonal God. He was fully engaged in our lives whatever season we were in. He loved me through my sin, my conflicts, my infantile attitudes, my marriage adjustments. He had not left us to fend for ourselves, to return when we were 'grown up.' I learned and keep learning that if the enemy succeeds in coming between me and God, he will succeed in gaining a foothold in my marriage.

Obviously, God loves you and will expose the enemy, like He did for me. But it's up to you to start believing God and quit believing the lies. You must quit giving him your ears and attention in the first place! Should he shout something in your direction, run to your Father, quit arguing with him.

The Word of God is your weapon. Dig into it and use it against the enemy. Know God's promises to you and your man. Challenge every crafty lie that comes your way. There's so much high sounding nonsense out there, and if you are not alert and careful, it will seep into your heart and marriage.

Paul told the church in Colossae in Collosians2:3-4,8 NLT

"In him (Christ) lie hidden all the treasures of wisdom and knowledge. I am telling you this so no one will deceive you with well-crafted arguments.. Don't let anyone capture you with empty philosophies and high-sounding nonsense that come from human thinking and from the spiritual powers of this world, rather than from Christ." (Brackets added)

As a wife, you will have to activate what singer and author Judy Jacobs calls "violent faith." She defines it as "sheer determination, aggressiveness in the Spirit, an attitude of perseverance, and raw gutsiness. It is a spirit of going against the norm, going against the tide, public opinion, perception, and sometimes even common sense."[2]

Let me explain how this worked out in our lives.

When Tommy and I were in the middle of conflict, I'd hear the mocking voice of the enemy roaring in the storm:

"Look at you, born again believers and you cannot even keep a good marriage! You are so angry at your husband right now. You are seated there plotting punishment and revenge. You are a horrible person! You think God is interested in people like you? You think there's any hope for your crazy little marriage?"

Previously I rolled over and took the beating. I thought it was the voice God, telling me how disappointed He was and trying to get me to repentance. But then God unmasked the enemy and began to urge me to take a stand against the negative voices screaming in my head.

So when I'd feel condemnation and guilt rolling my way, I began to say aloud:

"Oh yes, my husband and I are having issues, devil. But this is strictly between me, God and my husband. You are not welcome to spectate or talk. We three will handle it, we don't need you!"

And then I had to speak God's word instead of the fears and lies.

Don't just 'roll with the punches,' dear wife! Actively defy everything that is contrary to God's truth.

Getting Help for Yourself First

When you get on a plane, one of the first things they show you is how to put on the oxygen mask. In case of an emergency, you are supposed to put on your own oxygen first, before you try to do anything else or help another person.

It's a basic safety instruction; until you help yourself, you cannot help someone else.

When we apply the same basic concept to marriage, this is what it looks like: until you have been taught and tutored by God, until your own foundation is deep and stable, you cannot build anything with your spouse.

While God wants us to enjoy the extraordinary gift of friendship and oneness in marriage, we cannot create it on our own. We need Him.

We must thirst for Him and allow Him to tutor our hearts to love and care as He does. It's only when we have been changed and taught what "agape" love is that can we in turn pour out the same love to our husbands.

The essence of Agape is self-sacrifice. It is love which is of and from

God, whose very nature is love itself.[3]

Agape love is different from the love you feel towards your husband or for your family, because it's not based on feelings and emotions but involves choice. It did not feel good to hang on the cross but Jesus allowed Himself to be nailed to the cross because of His great love for us.

God wants to fill us with this kind of love so that we can in turn pour it out to our husbands.

I struggled with the idea of loving my husband in the agape-way because I did not understand how my will could override my feelings. I lived on the idea that "I feel, therefore I am!"

Eventually, God opened up 1 Corinthians 13:4-8 and Galatians 5:22, 23 and the verses gave me a glimpse of agape love.

1 Corinthians 13:4-8 says, "Love suffers long *and* is kind; love does not envy; love does not parade itself, is not puffed up; does not behave rudely, does not seek its own, is not provoked, thinks no evil; does not rejoice in iniquity, but rejoices in the truth; bears all things, believes all things, hopes all things, endures all things. Love never fails."

Galatians 5:22, 23 says, "But the fruit of the Spirit is love, joy, peace, longsuffering, kindness, goodness, faithfulness, gentleness, self-control."

The only way to love your husband this way is through God's enabling. When we step into agape love, we allow God to mould and grow us. We also give Him room to work on our behalf.

Winding Up

If there's one thing I want you to take away from this chapter, it's this; an extraordinary marriage comes from developing extraordinary intimacy with God.

Intimacy in marriage is like oil to the engine of your marriage car. It causes every other part to work well. Like Mary who broke the expensive jar of perfume over the Master's feet, brokenness will not go unnoticed or unrewarded. Some may scoff at it and your own flesh will resist it. But go with God anyway because that's the only way it works.

There's no greater depth to be found than between two people who have learned to fall in love with God and allowed Him to tutor their heart in the way of love.

I don't know how anyone weathers the early years without God's help. There are so many adjustments and new things to learn. I have needed God every step of the way. Without Him, I don't know where Tommy and I would be. Or if we would still be.

Ecclesiastes 4: 12 NIV says "Though one may be overpowered, two can defend themselves. A cord of three strands is not quickly broken."

God, you and your spouse are a majority. No matter what kind of blues and bumps come your way in the early years of marriage, you can have victory. Your relationship with God will power you through all of life's tough situations.

You may have been reading this chapter and you haven't even started your walk with God – you do not know Jesus as Lord and Savior of your life. You can do that right now.

The bible says

"For all have sinned, and come short of the glory of God." Romans 3:23 KJV

"For the wages of sin is death, but the gift of God is eternal life in Christ Jesus our Lord." Romans 6:23 KJV

Romans 3:22 NLT "We are made right with God by placing our faith in Jesus Christ. And this is true for everyone who believes, no matter who we are."

John 1:12 "But to all who believed him and accepted him, he gave the right to become children of God." NLT

If you want to give your life to Jesus, pray this prayer:

> *"Dear Lord Jesus, Thank you for dying for my sin. I know I am sinner and I need your forgiveness. I acknowledge that you died on the cross for my sin and rose again from the dead. Forgive me of my sin. Guide me and help me obey you and live for you. Thank you for all you have done. In Christ's name I pray"*

If you've prayed this prayer, please get a Bible and read it. Find a good Bible based church, pray and seek the community and friendship of other believers. Begin to live out what He's telling you. Your life and marriage will never be the same! You may also get in touch with me using the contacts at the end of this book. I would love to hear from you and pray with you.

Blues to Bliss

2

Building healthy expectations

"But always continue to fear the Lord. You will be re-
warded for this; your hope will not be disappointed."
Proverbs 23: 17b, 18 NLT

I came into marriage believing that my husband and I would always "get" one another. And even when we didn't, I thought that we'd somehow figure out a way to work things out - amicably, *easily* and *quickly*.

My hope quickly dissipated a few weeks into marriage as I began to see just how different Tommy and I were.

I was the in-your-face type of person, wanting to work through everything in a single sitting. My husband was quieter, ruminating and thinking type of person, preferring not to talk (especially not in the middle of the night).

I was born in the country and my dad was a contractor by profession - he built and created things with his hands. He brought up his sons to be the same way. And his daughters assumed that all men are handy men and can work miracles with tools and projects.

But Tommy grew up in the city and his father was a salesman. My husband was savvy and slick in many areas but handyman was not in his veins.

We clashed in our expectations and how we expressed (and did not express) ourselves. We wondered what was wrong with the other person and why our attitudes rubbed each other raw when we tried to resolve things.

We did not understand that everyone walks into marriage carrying silent ideas and thoughts on how their spouse should be.

All of us have some type of expectations we've put on our spouses. In fact most of us get married because we met someone who met and *exceeded* our expectations! And of course it's great to have, and continue to have expectations, like he will come home every night, he will love God, he will work a job and earn a living. That's healthy and needed.

But in our hopes, we fail to realize that expectations are only healthy when they are submitted to God. When we remove God from the equation and prop up our spouse on a pedestal, we set up our marriages for serious disappointment.

Roots of Unhealthy Expectations

We get in trouble when we begin to expect the man we married to give us something or be something they are not.

In my case, when we got into conflict, I wanted Tommy to talk to me and seem as interested in marriage as I was. His shutting down made me feel like he didn't care for me or our relationship. Talking, in my opinion, would not only help us resolve the issue on the table, but also make me feel secure and loved.

See my problem there? I wanted Tommy to supply something that only God could supply; unconditional love, worth and identity.

You might be reading this and thinking, "I don't expect my husband to replace God". Well, I encourage you to examine some of the things you want your husband to do and be for you, and how you respond when he doesn't.

Dealing with Expectations

Here are a few things we want to keep in mind when working through expectations in marriage:

1. Realize completeness comes from God, not your husband
Our upbringing, TV, friends, life experiences and personal beliefs influence what we think about marriage and what we expect from our mate. Again, not all expectations are bad. But God is quick to warn us in Jeremiah 17:5 that "Cursed is the man who trusts in man and makes flesh his strength, whose heart turns away from the Lord."

A human being cannot meet all the needs of another human being. We are not designed like that. So even as we expect certain things from our husbands, we need to understand that God is the Source. He might use our husbands as a channel but when the channel fogs up, we should stay focused on Jesus, the real Source.

When we are frustrated or disappointed in our expectation, we must see that for what it is; a symptom that we have put our faith in someone other than God.

I have grown to love the fact that God wired my husband differently. His weaknesses reveal my own larger weaknesses. Without his "failures," I would not see my tendency to put my hope in him instead of God.

At the end of the day, it matters not if your expectations are healthy. At some point they will go unmet because you married a human being. In those moments of failure, you must remove the burden from your spouse and see God.

2. Communicate your expectations.
Author and missionary Caleb Suko says,

"It's helpful to verbalize expectations mutually, in a way that's not demanding. For instance, you can first ask your spouse, "What kind of expectations do you have for me that I'm meeting or not meeting right now?" Then you could share your expectations. Even if you can't meet those expectations the process of verbalizing them to each other can be helpful on both sides."[1]

The thing about expectations is that we often fail to talk about them aloud. We generally hope our husbands will figure it out. But the shortest route to an unfulfilled expectation is keeping quiet.

I am an *Acts of service* girl[2]; I feel love through being served. Early in marriage, I expected my husband to delight me with service without being told. I wanted to be lavished with breakfasts in bed, creative dates, a clean house, laundry folded; all without having to tell him what I wanted.

Unfortunately my husband did not know his way around the kitchen. And he didn't (still doesn't) read minds.

I have learned thus; if I am tired and need help with dinner, I better speak up. Sometimes my guy will notice my tiredness and jump in to do what needs to be done. But if I truly need help, I am better off talking straight, instead of hoping he will somehow decipher my sighs or ambling walk.

Here's something else to chew on ladies. Men don't see things like we do. I mean that quite literally. They are not great at seeing minute tasks and details that need to be attended to.

I can't count the number of times my husband has failed to see things that are in plain sight. In fact, he likes to joke that I am an expert at hiding things in plain sight. Dinner might be right there in the fridge but he doesn't see it. Me? It's the first thing I see when I open the fridge! He's not being tedious or petty; he's simply not wired to *quickly* pick his way through a gazillion items.

So this means that when he's watching a game, you are better off not asking him to watch the dinner cooking on the stove as you paint your toe nails. Chances are he will miss something, most likely the food!

I hope you are catching the drift by now - understand your differences, give grace and express yourself!

3. Sometimes, you don't have to share all your expectations
I know I just said that we need to communicate our expectations. But there's a place and time for everything.

Recently, I was driving home on a new road and was climbing up the steep incline at about 50 miles an hour. As I drove up the incline, I suddenly noticed a road cutting right in front of me at the crest. Trucks and small vehicles were rumbling across the road. There were no signs on my road, no indications to slow down, no warnings. Just an intersection from nowhere. My foot flew to the brakes.

I neared the crest, heart beating. And to my dismay discovered that the "intersection" was actually a bridge! The cars were on top of the road I was driving on! But I could not see from a distance, because of my angle.

Expectations are a lot like that sometimes. Depending on where you stand, you can see all kinds of things and you hope your spouse is seeing them too. But many times we see different things even when we are looking at the same thing. Our views are colored by our upbringing, life experiences and what we think is true.

You might be seeing warning signs - a busy intersection - while he sees a bridge - no danger, no big deal, let's keep moving.

One husband says, "Even when I am sure (I am right) I am less adamant about my beliefs for two reasons. One, based on experience, I know I could be wrong. Two, even if I am right, offering grace to those who are "wrong" is God's will."[3]

Just because you have an expectation does not mean your husband has to jump on it. Or that it must be shared. Sift through your expectations and find out what is realistic and what is not.

Proverbs 10:19 NLT says "Too much talk leads to sin. Be sensible and keep your mouth shut."

Good word, right? Some things just require more growth out of *you*, not your husband.

4. You can't force change

Soon after communicating our expectations, many of us appoint ourselves as helpers. After all we are Help-meets, aren't we!

Dr Gary Smalley says, "You have the freedom and responsibility to change yourself, but not the other person."

You can't change your husband. That's God's job. Obviously, you need to discuss healthy expectations and communicate your needs. (More on communicating your heart in the Communications chapter ahead) But just because you have a legitimate need does not mean you can force your man to meet it. You may encourage him, but ultimately, he has to make up his mind to meet it.

Here's the good news – while you might not be able to change your husband, there's one person you can change.

You.

Work on you. Ask God to give you a better view of that intersection (or bridge). Ask Him to help you see things the way He sees them. Ask Him to help you love your husband with His agape love, whether he's doing what you want him to or not.

Adjusting Our Expectations.

Jesus, addressing the Pharisees, the teachers of law of His time, said,

"For the mouth speaks what the heart is full of. A good man brings good things out of the good stored up in him, and an evil man brings evil things out of the evil stored up in him." Matthew 12: 34b-35 NIV

The Pharisees were concerned with rules of law and keeping appearances. But they rejected the message of Christ which was about internal transformation that birthed external change.

We are a lot like the Pharisees. We fixate upon the outside, not understanding that our external behavior is rooted in our internal environment. What comes out of our mouths comes from what we have believed in our hearts. In order to change our words (which reveal our expectations), we must change what we have believed.

Maybe straightening out your heart and mouth sounds crazy considering where you are. Or at least where most of us started. You walked down the aisle carrying great hopes. You had your heart and mind straight then! And for a season, marriage seemed to be all that you hoped for.

Then the blues checked in. He stopped being the funny, tender guy you married. You started arguing about inane things. Money became an issue. Now you no longer see each other the way you used to. You are hurt and disappointed and certainly don't have the energy to do "one more thing" for your marriage.

You are not alone. Many wives, including myself, have walked that road. At some point, we've had to surrender (and keep surrendering) our thoughts and ideals and pick up God's truth.

Disappointment and pain does not happen to some people, it happens to *everyone*.

John 15:2 NIV says that "He cuts off every branch in me that bears no fruit, while every branch that does bear fruit he prunes so that it will be even more fruitful."

One way or another, you'll feel God's shears. He'll either be cutting off the dead things from your life or pruning the good so that you can bear more fruit. Don't be afraid when God comes to change you and what you believe about marriage.

In our early days, my husband and I would give each other the cold shoulder and not talk for days. I felt lost, forgotten and afraid. He felt alone, misunderstood, like a complete failure as a husband. Marriage got very hard. But it was hard because we held on to our selfishness and refused to change. It was difficult because we refused to create room for each other in our hearts.

It's important to be ready to do the hard work of changing from the inside, not just throwing some patch work on the outside. Be ready to say *"God it hurts so bad right now, but do your perfect will in me. Align my heart to your will. I don't want to keep burdening my husband and my marriage with things I shouldn't. Help me change."*

Sowing the Right Seed

God's word never fails. You always harvest what you put in the ground. It follows that if you want to reap a sweet marriage, you must plant sweet seed in the soil of your mind and heart.

Consider that the seed you put in the soil may not be visible for a couple of days or weeks. But after a while, something will pop out of the ground and manifest for everyone to see.

Proverbs 18:21 says "Death and life are in the power of the tongue, and those who love it will eat its fruit."

See that? You need to speak out the life that God is pouring into you. Your words must align accordingly! Ladies, some of us huff and puff when told to speak good things over our men. "Why, if he's lazy and good for nothing, then that's what he is, what do you mean I have to lie about it?"

Girl, I am not asking you to lie. I am asking you to speak faith!

Hebrews 11:1 says that faith is the substance of things hoped for, the evidence of things not seen. You have to reach into the realm of faith and begin to agree with God concerning your man.

The thing is, what you focus on, what you magnify, becomes greater, not less. The more you repeat what he seems to be (lazy), the more he becomes *it*. Your words do not motivate him to change, and neither do they motivate you to change your attitude towards him; you do not give life to the situation by speaking negativity and despair.

Instead, why don't you call those things that are not as though they are? What will you call your husband? Sure he might not be where you want him to be right now. But aren't you a Helpmeet? Aren't you supposed to encourage, lift up, support, see the positive and want good for your marriage? So what will you allow to come out of your mouth concerning your marriage?

Yes, sometimes you want to blow off because you are in pain and have had enough. But here's something worth remembering; as Martin Luther said you can't stop birds from flying over your head but you can keep them from making a nest in your hair.

The angry thoughts and pain might come to you but you don't have to give them life by saying them! You can rebuke them instead. Talk to God and ask Him to help you speak life, not death.

Your words have the power to direct the course of your marriage and can either usher in wedded bliss or keep you mired in your blues. Speak the Word of God concerning your situations, not what you feel. Take the higher position!

Here are ways to get our heads and hearts in order and sow the right seeds over our expectations for our marriage:

1. Believe God's word first.
You have to know what God says about your situation and believe it *first*. Because your victory and power lies not in peppy mind talks or positivity, but in God's Word!

James 1:5-6 NIV says "If any of you lacks wisdom, you should ask God, who gives generously to all without finding fault, and it will be given to you. But when you ask, you must believe and not doubt, because the one who doubts is like a wave of the sea, blown and tossed by the wind."

I love that about God - I don't have to be perfect, to have figured out everything in order to have a thriving marriage. I can come to Him "as is" and He heals and transforms me as we go along. He supplies my need at that moment of need!

That means that you don't need to have figured out everything in advance. But once He tells you the truth, you need to hold on to it and not waver.

As I write this I am going through a difficult season in the area of our dreams. My husband and I have been called to build peoples' capacities, through education, entrepreneurship, and partnerships, and we've believed God to see the dream come alive in bigger ways. But I have been hitting inner challenges and outside resistance. I've been feeling like I am not good enough. I am too quirky, judgmental, opinionated and critical. I feel like I am a hopeless mess and God has better people at His disposal.

The other day God told me that there's no cure for my humanity - this perfection I am aiming for does not exist. I will always need Him to help me overcome something. My weaknesses and sin? He makes that work for good too; they do not separate me from Him. Rather, they keep me dependent on Him. His love and affection, the oil to purpose, is not based on work, but on grace. His blessing in me and through me is not based on my abilities but my desire.

That's a message not just for this particular situation I am facing but for every situation we face in our marriages.

We will never have it all figured out. We don't have to understand all the ins and outs of marriage in order to have great marriages! Our emotions and minds don't have to be perfect for God to get with us!

Right now, it's okay if you don't know what to do about the bumps and frustrations of your marriage. It's okay because there's One who knows, and you can ask Him to help you figure it out. Don't do it by yourself.

Even when you think you know what you are supposed to do, make a habit of talking with God. He's the only One who knows the *why* behind things. He knows the intention and depths of our hearts. Only He can reveal them to you and direct the course of your actions.

We overcome the blues, not because we are perfect or strong, but because we are in relationship with One who is perfect and strong on our behalf.

2. Guard your heart, ears and eyes
A story is told of a man by the name of Charlie Stink who was con-

stantly being advised by his friends and co-workers that he should change his name. Finally he agreed, and went to court to have the process completed. The next day back at work, his associates inquired,

"What did you have your name changed to?"

"I changed it to George Stink," he answered, "but for the life of me I can't see what difference it's going to make!"[4]

Interesting how we can completely miss the point, huh?

An early-wed wife carries this huge bulls-eye on her back; she is a magnet for advice!

Can you think of some of the advice you received pre and post wedding? I bet not all of it was wonderful.

Before I got married, one married lady told me "Wait until you get married, that small waistline of yours will disappear!" Her voice carried such weight and drama and I wondered what I had done to elicit the comment. (It was the out-of-the-blues kind of comment). I thought it was a sweeping statement because she did not know my genetic make-up or eating habits.

Before you take me to task, yes some of us do gain weight after marriage and kids. But there are better ways of sharing such possibilities with single people.

What am I saying? You have to be careful about what you allow into your heart because it will affect how you think and what you expect out of marriage. Personally I allowed her words to momentarily fill my heart with fear. "Do I really want to get married?" "Marriage seems to have such drama, is it worth it?"

But at some point, I had to say *"Well, God has not given me a spirit of fear. And if I do gain weight, well, we'll just have to deal with it then"*

What things have *you* picked up? Maybe the reason you are stressing your husband to keep his wardrobe tidy is because your best friend regaled with stories of how her husband folds the laundry, irons his shirts and has a sense of style. Now you are mad at your man because he doesn't fold his clothes and has two left feet when it comes to style.

It's not that you can't listen to good stories and encouraging reports. But you can't import everything you hear because everyone's relationship is different. The only standard you need to be holding yourselves to is Jesus. Don't try to make your husband into something he's not simply because someone said it's a good thing.

3. Take personal responsibility for your actions and responses
Someone said, "Love is the thing that enables a woman to sing while she mops up the floor after her husband has walked across it in his barn boots."

Did you know that it's possible to "sing" in the midst of "mopping the floor" after your mate? When he's not done what you hoped he would, when he's hurt or disappointed you, it's still possible to give grace. I know that's easier said than done, but track with me.

Love begins and ends with *you* - what you think, what you believe, what you say.

When I got married, my natural reaction to our honeymoon blues was to wait for Tommy to change before I could do any changing of my own. I believed that my happiness and joy lay in his changing, not mine. True to that belief, I cried to God to change him and I played martyr, stayed completely miserable, as I waited for my answers.

I absolutely believed that as long as things were not going the way they should (that is, the way I wanted), I could not be happy. I pegged my ability to enjoy my marriage on circumstances outside my control instead of those within my control. Over time, I'd shockingly discover that Tommy could not be my happy-pill. He was my husband, not a pill. If I wanted happy, I had to go get it.

That's something you must do too; take personal responsibility for yourself. Take responsibility for your own dose of happiness and joy! Your husband is not responsible for you. Of course his behavior affects you. Of course he needs to do his part. But that doesn't mean he is responsible for your reactions and responses. What you chose to do with what he does or does not do is up to you!

Here's how it goes down in our house. My sweet man doesn't like house chores. I don't like them either, I've never been a fan of domestic chores. But the domestic end is my job, keeping the house falls under my turf (I am talking about my house now, not yours). Anyway, when my husband fails to clear away the dishes in the sink, after saying he will, I can get mad and blame him for my ensuing crazy mood. Or I can *choose* my response to his behavior. So what does this girl do? Sometimes I remind him about his promise, and he will get to it right away. Other times he doesn't get to it. Maybe there's a basketball game or he's just tired.

This girl has had to learn that an overflowing sink does not signal the end of the world. We can still hang out and enjoy the evening *with an overflowing sink*. Of course I am still hoping that he will get to the dishes the following morning, like he said he would. Sometimes he doesn't. You know, the clock. He oversleeps and he has to rush out to work. There again I have the option of walking around the whole day with my mouth dragging on the floor in anger. Or loading the dishwasher/hand washing the dishes myself. I have to think higher thoughts; *he did not do it on purpose. He meant to help but was overtaken by events.* I go ahead and remind myself of all the other times he's helped out.

I have learned to take this approach and apply it to other areas of marriage. I have learned that when I think the best of my husband, my response is always better!

Personal responsibility is an awfully big pill to swallow but it's a must if you want to change the dynamics of your marriage. We all want to blame somebody but lasting bliss doesn't perch on responsibility-phobic souls. Rather it takes root when we take personal responsibility of our actions and responses.

Winding up

It's important to have expectations in marriage but we must keep them at the feet of Jesus, not at the feet of our spouse. We must be filled with grace, be ready to give more than we receive, be ready to serve and change our minds.

#3

He speaks, she speaks but we are not communicating

"Conflicts are not a sign you've married the wrong person. They simply affirm you are human."

Dr Gary Chapman

"Your similarities, not your differences, will create some of your greatest fires in marriage"

I heard these words before I got married and couldn't believe how ridiculous the whole idea was. For me, the more Tommy and I were alike, the happier we were going to be! Being similar was not a bad thing, it was going to be the most amazing thing!

Two weeks into marriage and smack-a-dub in the middle of honeymoon, our similarities clashed. Our post-honeymoon itinerary included a one day getaway at a bush lodge outside the city and on the morning of our departure, something descended on my brand-new beloved husband.

Silence. Quiet. He shut down. On me!

Now you need to understand that I had just come off Courtship Highway, where I had been living on an exclusive diet of romance, sweetness, chivalry and words. His stillness knocked the air out of my newlywed chest.

But I recovered fast. And reckoned that if he could serve "attitude," I could serve it right back to him. In style. Boiling on the inside and hoping to punish him or guilt him out of his silence, I melted into icy silence myself.

But Tommy, who later confessed that he was going through serious inner adjustments to having a woman in his house, his bed and his life did not fathom the depth of my confusion, bewilderment or fear. He didn't notice my punishment either.

That's how many communication issues start and escalate. Two perfectly normal individuals suddenly start speaking in a language the other person does not quite understand.

In our case, Tommy melted into silence and hopes I get that he needs his space. I don't understand that and instead of finding out what's going on with him (hint, just ask!), I treat him the way he's treated me, but with a slightly different edge. I intend to hurt him the way he's hurt me. I hope my withdrawal will shake him up from his silence. He notices I am mad, but instead of righting the wrong, he withdraws further. I guess he doesn't want to mess with a livid bride. Either way his withdrawal makes me more mad. When I finally speak up, my words are filled with anger and resentment. And of course, my harsh emotions turn him off.

Miscommunication is a cycle and either person can choose to grow up and jump off the freakish ride at any time.

In a publication by the University of Florida, Deborah Humphries and Eboni J. Baugh describe the components of effective communication:

"Effective communication requires practicing the skills of listening and the expression of thoughts and feelings. It is much more than talking. Communication consists of verbal messages (what you say), contextual issues (how you say it), emotional tone (why you say it), and even non-verbal cues (what you don't say)."[1]

When you consider that most conflicts in marriage are a result of communication issues, you see why it's important to start developing communication skills early. The emphasis here is *learning and developing*. You don't get good overnight, but you keep practicing to get better.

When we are new at marriage, we can be mixed up in our communication. We are either hiding our true self or, the other extreme, emptying out without restraint. When you are hurt, disappointed or in pain, your instinctive reaction is not to open up. It's to hide and build up walls. We don't do it deliberately; in fact, many of us aren't aware of it until someone points it out.

But walls and facades don't create unity. You don't become one by running in the opposite direction of unity. Oneness and being of one mind demands openness, transparency, conversation and stripping of self.

I must reiterate this; without practical opportunities to learn and grow, we don't get better as spouses.

I love what Paul says in Hebrews 12: 11-13 NIV

"No discipline seems pleasant at the time, but painful. Later on, however, it produces a harvest of righteousness and peace for those who have been trained by it. Therefore, strengthen your feeble arms and weak knees. "Make level paths for your feet," so that the lame may not be disabled, but rather healed. "

The hurts and disappointments we experience are not meant to kill us but to grow us and make us better.

Keys In Communicating Effectively (And Breaking Down Those Walls)

1. Seek to connect, not just talk
John Maxwell says "everyone communicates, few connect."

If you are like me (and I am guessing you are, fellow daughter of Eve), you have better language skills than your beloved. It's not that he can't talk - there are many a men with hot debating skills too. I mean that as a woman, you have a sharper memory and hotter lips. You can go at your husband with a slew of words that are oiled and aided by a long memory, tepid emotions and desire to express yourself and win the conversation.

But when it comes to communication, especially during conflict, you need to understand that it's not about making a point. It's about communicating that point well, hearing his heart and coming to an understanding.

Proverbs 15:2 NIV says, "The tongue of the wise commends knowledge, but the mouth of the fool gushes folly."

Wise wife - Commends knowledge. Foolish wife - Gushes folly.

I can tell you that most wives don't set out to bag the foolish-wife medal. Everyone wants to be wise, smart, in control and in command of themselves and the situation. But then hubby comes along and does (or does not do) something and every ounce of wisdom and self control you have flies out of the window. At that point you feel like you have every right to express your feelings and thoughts and if it involves overriding better judgment, so be it!

But here's the thing dear wife - what comes out of your mouth can either encourage healthy conversation and connection or bring it to a screeching halt. You are responsible here. You can lead the conversation to a better place or towards the edge of a cliff.

As we said earlier, we are all learning these things and we'll make mistakes along the way, but we must be growing towards wisdom, not moving away from it. That means that when we blow it, we admit it, and then work on getting better.

Now that we are here, let me ask you a question: Have you noticed that your husband does not have a super-connected brain like yours? That he can't handle a flood of emotions and words? That whenever you fling tears and high emotions and roller-coaster actions at him at the same time, he kinda checks out?

Let me let you in on a secret that I've found to be true in my own marriage: It's not that he doesn't want to hear what you are saying, but he can't handle the way you are saying it.

You can be right all the way to the moon and back but unless you speak it with respect, the right attitude and wisdom, you will hit the same old walls.

2. Listening to your husband does not mean acquiescence
I like this quote attributed to Ogden Nash: "To keep your marriage brimming, with love in the wedding cup, whenever you're wrong, admit it; whenever you're right, shut up."

Love stays fresh and exciting as we work hard at *not* soiling and muddying it up. Yet muddling things up is something we are all familiar with.

Many marriages abide in long seasons of hot fellowship because one spouse, or both couldn't bear the thought of keeping quiet.

Take me, for example. I don't like being misconstrued. I like it when people know exactly what I think. So you know how that works out when my husband and I have differing opinions on something? I try to let him know exactly what's on my mind. You know, to save him all the trouble of figuring it out. But really, my true motive is to make sure he knows I have a differing opinion and I have every intention of sticking to it, no matter what he says.

Here's what I have been learning: zipping up when your husband is talking does not mean that you agree with everything he's saying.

I know that sped past some of us, so let me rephrase and dig a little deeper.

Giving your husband time to talk his mind, when you are trying to resolve something, does not mean that you are now in agreement with everything he's saying. It does not mean you lost all the power and he can do whatever he wishes from that point on. Rather, it means that you value and treasure him enough to draw out his heart. It means that you care about your lasting bliss, enough to do away with words, body language, facial expressions and inner chatter that try to steal it away.

Proverbs 25:24 NIV has this to say about the quarrelsome wife. "Better to live on a corner of the roof than share a house a quarrelsome wife."

The dictionary defines quarrelsome as "argumentative; contentious"

That means a multitude of words and thoughts and opinions roundly expressed without a lot of thought to the other person in the conversation.

Most men need time and space to process what their wife is saying. They don't handle interruptions, roller coasters and rabbit trails well. Most of us girls, we can swing by the moment. We can remember something he did last week and tie it to what he did this week and how that plays into the future. In other words, we can handle interruptions. But don't make the mistake of believing your husband is like that because he's not.

I am not talking about feigning meekness or being passive or shutting down your brain. You keep quiet so that you can practice *active* listening. Because no matter how agile and multi-talented we think we are, we can't talk and listen at the same time.

A couple of tips about active listening:

- It involves your whole demeanor, your body language, your facial expression; everything communicating "this is important" and "I want to understand what you are saying."
- You ask clarifying questions along the way. Instead of cutting him off, you might want to say, "This is what I understand by what you've just said, let me know if I have understood correctly..."

3. Swallowing your words won't give you a bad stomach

I took care of my nieces and nephews when they were young. On occasion, I'd feed them something they didn't like. Believe me they were not shy to express their displeasure. It came in form of spitting out whatever I put in their mouths. They didn't care about my shirt, or a clean floor or table. Mercifully, over the months and years and as they grew up, their eating habits changed... thank God!

It's easy to act like an infant when navigating honeymoon blues. He said something you don't like? Did something wrong? Out flies your opinion, all raw and crass and nasty and without care for the other person or sensitivity to the entire situation.

As I write this we have a little storm that's been hanging in the air for a couple of days. It's mainly me, I feel there's something that we need to address and I have brought it up and we've tried to address it. But we haven't completed the talking process and as at now, we don't know how to complete it. As far as I can tell, it might be one of those things where I need to wear my big girl pants and just grow up and overcome some internal angst and issues. I really don't know yet.

What I know is that at first, I wanted to just open my mouth and tell him everything I was feeling about what was going on. And maybe I did, a little. But the Holy Ghost arrested me and reminded me that "emptying out" - talking to just let off steam - without first addressing the root cause of my issues would take us backwards.

So I have had one of those weeks where I am more inward focused, working to find answers and healing for my frustrations. From God and not from Tommy. I am being reminded yet again why we need to watch our words. We are not at our best when we are worried or frustrated. Sometimes when navigating marriage blues, you just have to stay silent, not because you are not hurting or do not have an opinion or there's nothing to be said, but because you understand that you are not at your best and might not be looking at the situation objectively. You need more God-time, not talk-time.

As I've waited and prayed over the week, some things have become clearer to me. As they have, I have realized that my original thoughts and feelings about our situation still hold but there are better ways of saying them.

Which brings me to this; waiting to say something gives us time to process thoughts and feelings we'll never have processed had we rushed out of the door. As you process, you are able to phrase things in a way that your husband can understand and accept. That's the whole point of a conversation, right? To connect with him, not just talk. To find a solution, gain understanding and clarity. Unless you speak in a language he understands, a language that is devoid of disrespect, accusation and anger, he won't hear you. Neither would you, if the roles were switched.

Proverbs 18:19 says "A brother offended is harder to win than a strong city, and contentions are like the bars of a castle."

One careless word can set you back a thousand paces. Winning back your husband after careless talk is more work that holding down those careless words.

Proverbs 15:1 NIV says "A gentle answer turns away wrath, but a harsh word stirs up anger."

What you say or don't say can make the difference between escalating conflict or heading towards a solution.

I've seen it at work in my marriage when my husband meets my moodiness or tantrums with sweetness, affection and understanding. He doesn't start by pointing out how immature I am. He hugs me or does something sweet like fixing me a cup of tea or rubbing my back and gently asking "What is it Sweetie?" His warm reception always disarms me.

Paul put it really well in his letter 2 Corinthians 4:17 NLT "For our present troubles are small and won't last very long. Yet they produce for us a glory that vastly outweighs them and will last forever!"

The Holy Ghost is our ever present help in times of trouble and He will remind us what we need to do, when we need it. He will prompt you to avoid certain paths but it's up to you to obey!

4. Sleep over it. In the same bed.
It's not always possible to iron out all the creases the first time round. In fact, many times you might not even get anywhere near the first crease! Many young couples struggle with that because, first, they don't expect to have major storms in the early years of marriage and second, they think it's unchristian to have unresolved conflict hanging in the air.

Just so we are on the same page, I believe that we should seek resolution of conflict at the earliest possible opportunity. But that "earliest opportunity" might not be *now*, or even tomorrow.

God wants us to enjoy real peace in our marriages. Not fake peace that comes from sweeping things under the carpet or rushing through the process of resolution because we want to feel like "good Christians."

I struggled in my early months of marriage because I thought God wanted me to have all my ducks in a row *before* He could fellowship with me. So I worked hard to make it straight and get back to God's "good books." All this time, Tommy was at the receiving end of my crazy efforts and of course he was upset, because no one wants to be forced to do things they don't want to do.

I was busy trying to live out Ephesians 4:26-27 NIV "In your anger do not sin. Do not let the sun go down while you are still angry, and do not give the devil a foothold."

I guess I forgot that the sun goes down at about 6pm in Kenya and if we were up at 10 pm, trying to resolve issues because we did not want the sun to go down on us, well, we were a little late.

Here's what I am driving at; some issues will take time to marinate and resolve.

God doesn't mind you taking time to think over issues deeply. Unlike us, He is not merely interested in outward appearances. Neither is He threatened by processes or time. He is not seated in heaven twiddling His thumbs, wondering when we'll get our act together and stop giving His institution a bad name. He is interested in the conditions of our hearts, not just the condition of our marriage, and He will not relent until we are genuinely changed from the inside out. Heart issues are deep issues. He knows that, and we need to understand that too.

Just because you slow down does not mean you are standing still. Sleeping over it is not the same as becoming passive. Before you sleep over it, commit to something. You might say, "Can we talk about this tomorrow, I think I am too stirred up to discuss this right now" or "I need time to think this through. Can we talk about it (insert time)?"

Something might happen as you take time to think things through or calm down; you will be tempted to draw away from one another. You'll have to fight that urge to separate. That's what I mean by sleeping in the same bed.

Don't hang out in the living room watching TV till 4 in the morning. Work hard to keep the relationship going. You might not feel like kissing him when he comes home in the evening. Or fixing his breakfast the following morning. *Do it anyway.* Don't go with how you feel, go with what is right.

Those little sweet things you do when it's all sunshine in your house? Do them now when it's storming. You might not be able to do everything but do something. Seek to feed the 'connector,' not the 'separator.'

I mentioned how my husband and I have had an extended week of blues in our house.

A day or two ago, he woke up earlier than I did. Our typical morning routine includes hugs and kisses and goofing around. When I woke up I heard him moving around in the kitchen. I left the bed and was going to zip past the kitchen on the way to the living room. I wasn't feeling one bit of mush, I did not want to be close to him and a part of me wanted him to notice that I have given him a cold shoulder.

But knowing what I know now, I forced my feet to turn into the kitchen. I was all frosty and cool as I gave him a quick hug. At least "quick" was my intention. As I was pulling back, he drew me closer and whispered something funny into my ear, the same things we say to each other on normal mornings. I melted into his arms. For a few seconds anyway. It wasn't much but that small moment helped ease the tension in the air. We still had issues to sort out but the brief respite would keep the relationship going.

Whenever there are issues in marriage, I have learned that most husbands want to know they are still accepted, loved and wanted. It's what we want too, right?

But when you shut down completely, when you choose the couch instead of the bed, when you give him a cold shoulder in the morning because he was not so nice last night, you communicate that he's only loved and accepted when he is good.

The more you disconnect and feed those disconnecting habits, the deeper those negative grooves run in your mind. The hug in the kitchen didn't change everything for me, but it changed the tone and atmosphere in my heart.

Learning To Pursue Peace

You know how it goes. A huge elephant (simmering conflict) is sitting in the middle of your living room. You need to talk. But your husband is not ready to talk. For one reason or another, he has built up a massive stone wall and barricaded himself in an impenetrable cave.

So you sit there and believe it's your God-given duty as a Helpmeet to smash down the wall and make him talk.

You scale up those walls (force conversation) like a trooper. But within no time, you are falling back with bruised fists, a hurting heart and a very upset husband.

That was me early in marriage. I was scared and tired of our honeymoon blues - which were mainly in the communication department.

I was the straight-talking we-can't-sleep-till-we iron out-our-differences bride. He was the quiet we-don't-have-to-talk-about-this-now-or-ever-so-leave-me-alone new groom. The more he resisted talking, the more I pushed for it. The more he withdrew, the more I ran after him.

About 6 months into marriage, I cried this into my journal, a revelation from God:

"I should not make him dance on his lame foot. Push the buttons of his

strength, not his weaknesses."

At that point God had been showing me that my communication style was wanting, to say the least. Making a big deal out of my husband's weakness (inability to communicate) was not going to usher us to bliss-land. Sure, he had personal challenges to overcome - he needed to learn how to stop avoiding conflict.

However, my jumping up and down on his handicap, demanding that he overcome it so we could be happy, was not helping the situation. When you have a wound and want it to heal, you don't poke, prick and pick at it. You back off and give it time to heal. When you touch it, you are tender and careful in your ministrations.

God was telling me, "don't pick at the scab, don't force your husband to talk, keep the peace."

Over time, God would open up the next level and show me how to *pursue* peace, not just how to keep it.

Maybe you are wondering "What's my job then, am I supposed to stand there and do nothing? Am I supposed to pretend we are okay and everything will get back to normal by itself? Cos you know that won't work at my house! I am the conversation initiator and if I do nothing, nothing gets done!"

Well, your job is to change yourself, with the help of the Holy Spirit. God's job is to change your husband. Make no mistake, God wants you to have real peace in your house. He doesn't want you to ignore the elephant in the room, because that's not how He wants us to operate. But at the same time, He doesn't want you hurting one another in the name of communication.

Psalm 34:14 says "Turn from evil and do good; *seek peace and pursue it.*"

The reason God wants you to stop forced communication is so that He can teach you how to inspire real connection.

God is interested in both of you, not just one of you. When you pray, God will be working inside you as well as your circumstances. I can tell you from experience that the more I pressed in with God, the more opportunities I had to have sane, calm conversations with my husband. The more I emptied out to Him the more He filled me with the wisdom and courage I needed to run the full course.

I don't know how God will create those opportunities for you, but I know He will create them when you press into prayer and relationship with Him. You might find that you have grace to press past the same communication barriers that previously knocked you down. You will be seeking a good time and place to have conversation, instead of mouthing off the moment he walks through the door. You'll be patient enough to serve (see, you cooked for him!) dinner and will be on the lookout for those "moments of peace" when he's relaxed.

You might say to him "Honey I want to talk about (insert the issue), can we talk about it now? Or when else is a good time?" You will go ahead and seek a commitment to a time and day. And you'll hold him to his word. When that time comes, you will bathe your words with grace and mercy, not pointing fingers or casting blame. You'll be careful to keep your words short and to the point, continuously asking God to help you with your emotions.

You might stumble and fall and not perform perfectly. Just remember that real life and real marriage is messy, it's not a performance. Don't give up. Remember that every opportunity, even the ones where you fail, is an opportunity to work on *your* growth. Be quick to notice your own progress because that will encourage you to be better next time.

5. Get with God
It doesn't matter what is going on the outside, God is always more concerned with what is going on within you. He is interested in changing you, more than He is in changing your spouse (to suit your needs) or fixing the situation. So you'll want to be praying more than you are talking.

Most of my "prayers" in those early days were just sobs and massive amounts of tears. It wasn't calm, collected, mature prayers but messy in every sense. But I learned that it was better to cry and wail at the feet of Jesus than to be off somewhere weeping by myself.

Wherever Jesus is, there is hope, but alone, there was only despair. I did not need words or eloquence because God can decipher every prayer and type of agony.

As you get with God, He will begin to surface the motives and intentions of your heart. They might not be massive bolts of revelation, just soft nuggets of truth rising from your brokenness and pain. He will comfort and affirm you and surface the roots of dependence and the expectations you've placed on your husband. Pull back and let His light shine into your heart and illuminate the places you need to change.

Don't try to hammer your points home. Connect with the only One who can change your husband and allow Him to work in you and work in him.

6. Ask God to reveal to you what makes your husband uncommunicative

Just because your husband struggles to communicate does not mean he doesn't have anything to say.

We wives like to fill in the gaps when our husbands take long to share their minds. Just observe couples in group settings and you will notice how some wives have perfected the art of speaking for their husbands, "clarifying" everything their husband says.

Don't be that wife. Don't assume you know why your husband is struggling. Don't fill the gaps with clever deductions. Even if you think you know why he's pulling away, you really don't know his heart. Only God does.

Make a beeline for his Maker instead of being satisfied with your own clever deductions. Ask God to show you the root cause of his struggles and how to pray for him.

God might begin to show you areas that have got nothing to do with your conflict and as you pray with understanding, not just assumptions, you will begin to see real progress and healing.

7. Persevere

"We have loved each other in the manner the other deserves. We have given and handed out portions in equal measure to what we have received from the other. We have not loved as Christ loved us. We have been competing, building high walls instead of laying it all down for one another. Fears, anxieties and disappointments have made of us two opposing armies, instead of being one unit moving forward and soldering tough times together. Now I see that we must not treat each other as we both deserve. But as Christ expects. We must come out of "loving" behind individual stonewalls, from where we converse, carry out marriage business, throw pebbles and stones, throw crumbs of love at each other. We must love each other the way Christ expects, not the way we deserve."

An excerpt from my journal from my early months of marriage.

At this point God had just delivered me from the "spirit of giving up." I was exhausted, trying to work on our blues and I told God "I quit, I've tried everything and it doesn't work".

I had no idea what I was giving up, but I felt things had to change.

And it was at this point when I felt God ask quietly, "Have you talked to his pastor yet?"

My husband wasn't terrible, only incredibly withdrawn and at this point, God wanted me to know we were not alone. That there was always a way out as long as we didn't give up!

Since then I have learned that successful marriages are not the prerogative of the brilliant. Rather anyone, even the seemingly disadvantaged, can have success as long as they work hard and refuse to quit.

As you work on your communication blues, you must come to that place where you refuse to quit. You must dig in your heels and refuse to give up on God.

There's this one beautiful thing that will keep you moving even as you work to better your communication: *Focus on the rest of your marriage.*

It made a huge difference in my marriage. Previously, I would camp on what was not working and would base my whole relationship around it. One small issue would occupy my mind and influence my behavior. Over time God would teach me that it's very hard to ignore a good friend but it's very easy to ignore a nagging wife. So I was better off working on being my husband's friend. And not just in the good times but especially in bad times.

So don't neglect what is working in your marriage. Don't take his not talking as an excuse to stop working on your general relationship. If he's coming home to you every night, paying the bills, going to church, celebrate that.

Continue living; serve him, go out on a date. Yes the "unresolved" undertone will still be there. But keep moving forward anyway. The more you focus on what is working the more your marriage will tilt towards the positive.

8. Keep working on yourself and die to pride
"If a person will spend one hour a day on the same subject for five years, that person will be an expert on that subject." Earl Nightingale

We can all become an expert at ourselves because we spend the most time with ourselves. As you work on your communication, understand that the only person you are responsible for is you. God won't hold you responsible for your husband's actions or inactions but He will hold you responsible for yours.

As we've said throughout this book, directly or indirectly, God is after you. He holds the world in his hands, including your husband, and you don't need to help Him. The person you are to be most concerned about is you. Your reactions, your responses, your thoughts, your words and your behavior.

I mentioned earlier that God asked me to reach out to my mentors when we began having difficulties in marriage. One of the things I had to overcome at that moment was pride.

You know how as newlyweds you want everyone to think you are okay? Yeah, that.

Plus, I did not want to tell the very people who had poured into us that we were having difficulties when they had done a stellar job preparing us for marriage. I did not understand that the reason they prepared us was because challenges would come! And when they did, we could walk through their open doors unashamed.

So be ready to die to the flesh and its pride and desires. As you pray and trust God, He will lead you to do uncomfortable things. Like involving your mentors or pastors, for example. You must be ready to push beyond "normal" and do what God tells you to do.

9. Have regular preventive maintenance
Let me be honest with you and say that at our house, I am the one who is more interested with "preventive" talks. "How are we doing" talks are not my husband's cup of tea.

As wives we *feel* better when we *know* our relationships are working well. Most men are not feely and relational by nature and therefore they don't always see the little bumps and creases of the relationship. And even when they do, the little bumps and creases don't bother them as much as they bother us.

I am not letting husbands off the hook. In fact one of our mentors is a strong believer in husbands taking the lead here. He has told my husband on more than one occasion to take me out for a date and initiate the "How am I/we doing?" kind of discussions. So yes, I do come from the school of thought that husbands take the lead *everywhere*.

But my point is that it's learned behavior for most guys. You are the one with the genes and disposition. And the Helpmeet title. You are a team and share equal weight in this marriage deal. I am saying that to encourage you if you feel like the scale tips on your end when it comes to checking up on your marriage.

It's a silly driver who waits for the car engine to conk out before he takes the car to the mechanic. You are a partner in marriage; you are in the driver's seat as much as your husband is.

So go ahead and pick a relaxed time, when, say, you are out on a date. When things are good between the two of you so that the questions are not be mistaken for nitpicking. Don't make a whole production out of it. Make it part of your natural conversation, part of your daily life and interactions. That way, you will deal with things before they become big problems.

The Boundaries of Peace

In their book "Boundaries in Marriage, "Authors Henry Cloud & John Townsend say,

"Things don't change in a marriage until the spouse who is taking responsibility for a problem that is not hers decides to say or do something about it."[2]

When one of us decides to take action, it gives opportunity for uncomfortable things to be brought up and the light of God to illuminate our actions and thoughts. As you work on your communication blues, you will eventually address the unhealthy undertones in your communication and put boundaries and rules for healthy communication.

For example if in the past he has yelled or walked out in the middle of a conversation, you want to call that out. "I want you to know that I feel disrespected when you walk out in the middle of conversation".

You seek to lay boundaries not just for your own protection but to create room for him to take up responsibility. In my marriage, I was all over the place, trying to fix every problem in our marriage, so much that my man had no idea where to step in. When I began to pray more, talk less and put some of these lessons into practice, his space became clearer and we made progress in communication.

So let it be clear between the two of you that you will no longer carry each other's burdens. There will be consequences to actions. If he shouts, you are no longer obligated to continue with that conversation. If you shout, he's not obligated to continue either. If he refuses to talk, you will not be running after him. Everyone will have to grow up. There will be mercy and grace but there'll also be consequences to unhealthy behavior.

Winding Up

When it comes to developing good communication and conflict resolution skills in your marriage, don't forget these 4 things:
- Always remember the goal of the conversation, don't be sidetracked.
- Be proactive, don't wait for small things to become big things before you start a conversation about them.
- Remember that even the most well-intentioned talk can head south if the timing and place is wrong.
- It's easier to talk to a friend – work on building the rest of your marriage, especially your friendship.

4

Submission and leadership; bursting the myths

I want my husband to lead me and our family. But in order for him to do that I must be willing to submit to his lead... I must surrender my grip of control and self-ish ways and trust him!"

Jennifer Smith.

Many of our worldviews on gender roles are formed (albeit subconsciously) very early in life. During my teen years and early adulthood, I nurtured hot and confused ideas about what it meant to be a woman.

I was the quintessential tomboy growing up. I dressed like a boy and was often confused for one, with kinky hair, scrawny frame, scruffy knees and dirty shorts. It wasn't just physical - in my dressing and looks - it was also in my mind.

I wanted to be a boy because I believed women were getting a raw deal in our highly patriarchal African society. While men were calling all the shots, the women, who seemed to be doing all the hard work at home, were subservient and powerless. In my mind, being a man would afford me all the power and control they seemed to wield so effortlessly.

My dad was my hero and I loved him to pieces. I was needy and fussy, ever seeking his attention. I wanted to know he loved me, was proud of me, liked me and accepted me. Like many kids, my nagging disposition was just a manifestation of what was going on within me. Over time I'd discover that the desire to "rule like the guys" really came from that hole in my heart that I wanted daddy to fill. I have no doubt my dad loved me. But he was from a different generation - he communicated his love and devotion through tough discipline, provision, keeping his distance.

That's where God found me at the age of 21; utterly confused, working hard to be noticed and appreciated by others, especially those in authority, believing performance led to acceptance, secretly despising males (and their authority), but craving the power and control they had.

Over time, God would heal my heart and fix its many broken pieces.

From hindsight I am glad I got married "late" because there was so much to deal with! (Now I didn't say *you* are unmarried because you have issues, so don't send me letters!)

Eventually though, marriage began to stir up the pains and wounds of my past. I found myself where many wives find themselves as newlyweds. You've heard about submission and you know all about your husband's mandate to lead the marriage. But because of wounds, baggage, pain and unhealed sorrows from childhood and life experiences, submission becomes a painful and difficult ordeal. Or, in many cases, you think you are submitting but it's a broken kind of submission, not the healthy submission espoused by the Bible.

The funny thing is, sometimes you can't tell exactly what you believe - from deep within, not just lip service - until you become a wife. You think you've clearly understood submission until out of the blues he says he doesn't like your favorite pink blouse, because "it's too low cut". At that point, what you truly believe pours out.

Unless we properly understand the God-ordained roles of submission and leadership, we'll struggle in marriage and find ourselves turning the wheels in blues-land.

What Does The Bible Say?

Ephesians 5:21-27 NIV *"Submit to one another out of reverence for Christ. Wives, submit yourselves to your own husbands as you do to the Lord. For the husband is the head of the wife as Christ is the head of the church, his body, of which he is the Savior. Now as the church submits to Christ, so also wives should submit to their husbands in everything. Husbands, love your wives, just as Christ loved the church and gave himself up for her to make her holy, cleansing her by the washing with water through the word, and to present her to himself as a radiant church, without stain or wrinkle or any other blemish, but holy and blameless."*

Don't you love how God begins the famous "submission" verses? Look at Verse 21. We are to submit to *one another* out of reverence for Christ. Submission is not just a prerogative for wives, but for husbands too. Submission for husbands typically manifests through tender leadership. It involves listening to her and taking into account her thoughts and input as he steers the home.

The rest of the verses go on to describe the wife's mandate to submit to her husband as the head and the husband's mandate to love his wife as Christ loved the church.

Many times women will ask, "Why do we do have to do all the submission, that's not fair!" I felt that way for many years, until I began to realize that God did not ask women to submit to all men, only to their husband. Moreover, God was not taking volunteers on the day he carved out roles for the man and woman, so maybe it's time we quit crying over something we had no control over and accept what we got (a sweet deal) and trust His purposes.

The roles of leadership and submission serve and reveal an *eternal* purpose.

God created us for fellowship (Revelation 4:11) and to have dominion over his creation (Genesis 1:28). For the latter part to happen there has to be some type of order. You can't have two heads, someone has to lead. There has to be a "governor" and it begins in the smallest unit; the family. God's desire in creating marriage was that it would reflect the kind of relationship He has with us, through His Son Jesus as the bridegroom and the church as the Bride.

Let me let you in on something, sisters. Loving leadership is a heavy responsibility. Think about it, when was the last time God asked you to love someone to death? That's exactly what Christ did for the Church and what He instructs husbands to do for their wives.

A husband puts it this way: "God did not say men could be the head if they felt like it, or if their wife signed on. God expects men to lead, regardless of how they or their wife feel about it. This (leadership) is a "Just Do It" kind of thing![1]

Most husbands are not walking around cockily, feeling all qualified and wanting to lord it over their wives. If anything, those who truly understand their role wish the load was lighter.

Before we get into specifics, let's get one more thing out of the way.

God loves *both* man and woman, *both* husband and wife, equally. Our roles have got nothing to do with our value. Oh, how I struggled with that. I thought God loved men more because He gave them all the power, and they could do whatever they wanted with it. But that's not true. God loves us equally. No one is free to do whatever they want with the power and responsibility God gives.

It breaks God's heart when people abuse authority and power. He wants leaders and heads to lead and love as He does - sacrificially and tenderly. There's mercy and forgiveness for those that have misused or abused power, when they repent. But God is also a righteous God and that means that judgment will come to those who do not.

If you have been hurt or abused, God does not approve of it. St. Augustine said "Never judge a philosophy (or truth) by its abuse". Just because people abuse power and authority does not mean God approves of it. God loves you. He hurts for you and wants to heal you.

Overall most women don't go through abuse or intentional misuse of power in the home. We are just brought up in imperfect homes, by parents who have their own luggage and wounds from the past. Dads are human beings too. They fail. We can't hold on to their failure and spend the rest of our lives pining over what they did or did not do. We must turn to God for hope, healing and restoration. He heals the broken heart, restores that which was lost and makes all things new.

The Ephesians Mandate: Understanding Headship

Typically, when we talk about submission and headship, we start with the ladies. But what does it mean for the husband to provide loving leadership in the home?

I must clarify that this section is for your understanding as wives, since it is you I am writing to. Don't read it and 'bookmark' it for your husband to read! I know husbands will read this too, and I am grateful for that.

But I do not want wives to take this portion (or any part of this book) and use it to start "I told you so" battles in their home. Instead, read it, meditate and pray and use wisdom to apply what you are learning.

Again, and we'll cover this later in more detail, it doesn't matter if your husband is being the leader God wants him to be. It's not your responsibility to make him. Encourage, support, yes. Force and coerce? No, that's not your job.

With that out of the way, let's go back to our Scriptures. Ephesians 5:25 gives this command "Husbands, love your wives, just as Christ loved the church and gave himself up for her."

Headship can be defined as *"the divine calling of a husband to take primary responsibility for Christ-like servant leadership, protection, and provision in the home."*[2]

Your husband's primary responsibility is to love you as Christ loved the church. Whether that's paying the bills, making sure you're all going to church or loving you, it springs from that responsibility of servant leadership that Christ demonstrates.

Here are some key takeaways from the "Ephesians Mandate:"

1. Leadership is about responsibility, not power
Husbands are commanded to love their wives the same way Christ loved the church. How did Christ love the church? He died for her. His headship has got everything to do with responsibility, not power. Loving leadership nurtures, protects, goes out of its way and seeks the good of those under its wing. It does not demean, belittle or lord over.

2. A husband is to love his wife sacrificially & tenderly
Verse 25: "In this same way, (i.e the way Christ loved the church and died for her) husbands ought to love their wives as their own bodies." (Brackets added)

While a loving husband will value his wife as an equal partner, he also recognizes that his bride is more than a partner, she is a precious treasure.

Wives, do you know what it means to be a precious treasure? It means that you *act* like one. This calls for you to leave room for him to love you tenderly and sacrificially. You celebrate chivalry, allow him to kill the bugs and open the doors for you. In your busy one-track, got-to-get-it-done-yesterday mode, you slow down and make room for him to shine.

See, there's nothing wrong with being a weaker vessel - you are designed differently, so that you and him complement one another. You are feminine, he is masculine. There's nothing shameful about Christ dying for the church. I don't hear the church raising a raucous because Christ was loving her sacrificially - we accept His death and sacrifice as a precious gift to us.

And so should you as a wife, accept your husband's love, sacrifice and tenderness. Encourage it, revel in it, let him know how much you need and appreciate the extra ways he loves you. Be careful to notice his sacrifices.

3. He is to be responsible and intentionally invest in his marriage
When my husband and I were courting, he was on top of his game; he was effusive, sweet, tender and romantic. He pursued me like a lion chasing a gazelle. Not to eat me thankfully, but to have me in his life.

Most men are on top of their game when they are pursuing a girl. (If you are reading this and are single and have a man who doesn't have his woo and pursue game on, sweet sister lace up your shoes and run for your life. If he won't pursue you now, he won't pursue you in marriage).

A husband has to make *intentional* effort to pursue his wife after marriage. It's a difficult thing, to pursue what he already has but that's one of the ways he leads her and stays intentionally invested in his relationship. Love is not passive, and wives are wired to respond to active love.

Many husbands soon discover that the investment and commitment their wives are looking for - the woo and pursue thing - is not found in the big things, but the small seemingly-unimportant things. Like asking about her day (and listening), preferring her above something he likes, helping her, arranging for a date, generally finding out what makes her tick. And then giving it to her.

4. He understands that the enemy is after him as the head of the home and is willing to fight

As leaders, husbands are the first line of defense for their marriage and home.

The enemy has waged war on men for centuries and many have succumbed to his fiery darts. But many more have stood and gallantly fought for their marriages and homes. It's a huge responsibility, standing up when society and popular culture, even your own weak flesh, wants you down.

I tell my husband this all the time - I love hearing him walk around the house whistling or singing, or snapping his fingers to a silent tune in his head. There's something about his relaxed happy demeanor that speaks a deep peace and rest to my soul. My dad, a carpenter by training, used to fix things around the house with a whistle or song on his lips. My most precious memories of him are of a hammer pounding away in the afternoon heat and a whistle rising above the din. There's something powerful about a whistling dad, a happy husband, a peaceful man. He gives life to everyone and everything around him, especially his closest and dearest. That's how God made men, to be leaders in the home. To be protectors. To inspire life and greatness to those under their care.

But to get to these "simple" things, - e.g a whistle that changes the atmosphere in the home - a husband has to overcome inner challenges and set a high standard in his own life. He cannot take his relationship where he has never been. He doesn't have to be perfect, but understands the responsibilities he's been charged with. And to lead and love well, he works hard to be well first. He digs deep into his relationship with God and seeks answers for the deep questions of his soul. He fights fear and passivity. He fights to keep a guard over his eyes and heart and mind.

As a wife, the more you understand the warfare he's involved in, the more you will stay on your knees, praying for him.

5. He tries to understand he's not her answer

All of us wives come into marriage with one type of scar or another - for some it's just a small knick where an old boyfriend broke your heart. For another it's a still-healing wound from childhood. Yet another wife might be grappling with a gaping wound that no husband-salve will heal.

No matter the depth of a scar or the general pull to fix his wife, a loving husband understands he cannot fix her inner blues and sorrows. He's patient, supports and encourages healing and growth, but learns to lead and pray her towards the right direction. The direction of her Savior.

6. He understands that it doesn't have to be perfect

For both husband and wife, learning the way of marriage - of loving leadership and submission - is a process, not an event. A man who wants his marriage to soar does not wait for leadership to be perfect before he offers it. He does not give up on leadership even when efforts go unrewarded. He does what needs to be done, even when it appears as though he's alone. He purposes not to measure his growth and value by how much appreciation he gets from his wife, but by what the Lord expects from him. He presses through even when the journey is painstakingly slow, difficult and imperfect.

7. He's willing to learn leadership

Leadership and steering a home is something most men learn as they walk the highway of marriage and life. Unfortunately, we don't understand this in the early days of marriage. Most men and their women want to hit the ground running, perfect on Day 1. Unfortunately, this is an unreal expectation. Leadership is a skill, habit and grace that's learned and refined over time. A husband needs to be willing to go through the process; learning, falling, rising to his feet again, trying again, never quitting.

These keys are summarized aptly by Matthew Henry in his Genesis commentary: "The woman was made of a rib out of the side of Adam; not made out of his head to rule over him, nor out of his feet to be trampled upon by him, but out of his side to be equal with him, under his arm to be protected, and near his heart to be beloved."[3]

Now, some of us might read this section and think "that's so idealistic" or "my husband is nothing like that". I want you to consider that last point - loving leadership is learned.

Consider also your challenges when it comes to laying down your will and becoming united with your husband. It's a journey. The same way you learn and perfect submission over a lifetime is the same way he will learn and perfect headship over a lifetime.

That said, we'll explore some ideas later on what to do if you are in this difficult position.

But first, let's look at submission in marriage.

The Role of Submission in Marriage

Submission can be described as *"the divine calling of a wife to honor and affirm her husband's leadership and help carry it through according to her gifts."*[4]

Broken down, submission means supporting, honoring and respecting my husband as the sacrificing leader of our home. It means deferring to him on those occasions we can't come to a mutual decision, but a decision is needed immediately.

Obviously, it's easy to 'submit' to a man when he's in full pursuit mode. He's sweet, thoughtful and romantic and you can't fathom not ever wanting to follow his lead.

And then you marry him.

And the finer points of his personality begin to emerge. He no longer hangs on to your every word. He can't put his clothes where they are supposed to be. He likes the TV remote too much. He's not as perfect and wonderful as you thought when you were courting. The result? The last thing you think he needs is "submission,"; he needs someone to set him straight! And who better to do it than you?

I know this because I have been learning to submit to my husband for all our 6+ years of marriage.

Having grown up in a strict traditional African home, I learned to live by my parents' strict rules. In secret, I could mumble, complain and get angry all I wanted, but in the end I did what was expected.

So I came into marriage having perfected the art of silent rebellion. Mercifully, by the time I met my husband, God was already working deeply to bring healing to the broken areas. But I still had a long way to go - I could talk about submission in theory without throwing a fit, but carrying it out in practice, well, that was the journey.

The earliest opportunity to submit to my husband came on our wedding day. We had just had a glorious wedding ceremony and in the afternoon party, a guest stood up to share some words of wisdom and present gifts to us.

A few minutes into his speech, I felt we needed to move closer to the guest, in order to be in a better position to receive the gifts. My foot was in mid-stride when I heard my husband ask where I was going.

"To receive the gifts," I answered, surprised. (Wasn't it obvious that we were standing too far?)

"Let's wait," he answered with a gentle new-groom smile, "He has not called us forward yet."

No one saw the twitch on my face. Or the small tufts of smoke beginning to curl from my ears. But Tommy may have noticed the flick of chin and the stiffened back.

I could not believe he had just cut me down in front of people.

I recovered quickly, put back the smile (and foot) and stood by his side. But inside I was boiling. It was the first time, but not the last time I'd follow his leading on the outside while screaming and resisting on the inside.

Please note, I could have explained to my husband why I thought we should move closer to the speaker, instead of getting mad and clamming up. So by all means, submission doesn't mean not expressing your mind and following blindly. You need to talk and explain your thoughts.

Understanding Helpmeet

One of the reasons we struggle with submission is because we don't understand the role of 'helpmeet.'

Genesis 2:18 KJV "And the LORD God said, It is not good that the man should be alone; I will make him an help meet for him."

The original Hebrew word for "help" is *ezer*, which means "one who helps". The word *ezer* is used many other times in the Bible and it refers to God as our helper. For instance, when David said in Psalm 54:4 "The Lord is my Helper," he uses the word *ezer*.

Women are not men's helpers in the sense of being more powerful, like God is. The full word "help meet" - *ezer kenegdo* - renders a more accurate meaning.

Kenegdo means "counterpart to" or "equal to matching." Thus, we see that the woman is a fitting partner to the man; equal in strength, power and value. Adam rejoices at their similarity in Genesis 2:23: "This is the bone of my bone and flesh of my flesh."

As a woman, you are not a rank lower than your man and he's not a rank higher than you. Rather, you complement one another. Together, you accomplish what you can't accomplish apart.

When you think about your hands, both of them are equal but opposite. Together, you can do tasks which you wouldn't be able to do with one hand, or with two hands that are the same. [5]

You are better together than apart.

What Submission is Not

Let's go ahead and debunk a few misconceptions about submission:

1. It's not gritting your teeth and making yourself follow his lead

When submission is hard, the easiest compromise is to "just do what he wants". Case in point, my wedding day. I did not agree with my husband, but instead of starting a brief discussion (as far as it was possible, seeing that we were standing in front of a crowd) and sharing why I thought we needed to move closer, I clenched my teeth and did what I thought was the "submissive" thing. But it was a show - I did the right action, but inside, I nursed the opposite attitude.

The Bible is filled with examples of instances where people honored God with their lips or actions while their hearts were far away from truth. You can find examples in Isaiah 29:13, 1 Samuel 15:13 - 35.

In 1 Samuel 15, King Saul tries to lie to Prophet Samuel concerning carrying out the Lord's command to destroy the Amalekite nation. God had instructed Saul to destroy *everything* but instead King Saul keeps the best of the animals and spares the life of Agag, the Amalekite king. God reveals the sin to prophet Samuel and the prophet confronts Saul about his disobedience.

Because of his sin, the kingdom is torn away from King Saul and given to another.

True submission is not merely doing or saying the right things but about embracing the *whole command of the Lord from the heart.*

Like all the Lord's commands, sometimes practice is what begins to make "perfect." In other words the beginning of obedience can be a struggle but the struggle shouldn't overcome our determination to do the right thing.

Many times wives learn submission by way of submitting, not before. It's a journey, and God desires that we invite him into our struggles and have Him help us rather than fake our way through it.

He loves for me to wrestle through something my husband has asked rather than have me grit my teeth, shut down my brain and do the "wifely" thing on the outside.

Wrestling through submission doesn't strike us as the right recourse because we tend to esteem outside actions above inner attitudes and motives. After all, our hearts are not out there on display, and people can't tell what's going on in our hearts.

However the key to true victory in this area is inviting God into the midst of our pain and struggles and allowing Him to help us. The opposite is hypocrisy; outside 'obedience' that covers up inner rebellion.

Hypocrisy and pride cover up sins that need to be repented of and wounds that need healing. Marriage is one of God's refining instruments. In marriage our sins and needs are laid out in the open. As children of grace, we are to fall at His feet and trust Him to change us, not run off and try to fix ourselves, or worse still, pretend that our issues don't exist.

God wants you to wrestle through your pride, ego and wounds. He wants you to bring your struggles to Him so that He can heal you. He is interested in your lasting bliss, more than you think; He is the Author of your marriage and wants you to succeed!

Learn to lean into your pain. Those moments you feel your heart racing in the opposite direction of unity with your husband, turn to the Lord. Don't mask your struggle. Ask for wisdom and strength and a heart that trusts His plan for marriage. You can't *feign* your way to a strong marriage, you *work* yourself there. That journey begins by being brutally honest about the condition and attitude of your heart.

Now a caveat, there are many times when you will submit without really having all of yourself on board with that decision. As I said, it's a journey and honestly, the journey will not end on this side of the sun. I am not suggesting that submission should be a breeze. You can expect some sort of discomfort every time you crucify the flesh. But I am saying that once you decide to unite with your husband, there will be some kind of peace that comes with that decision. You won't be nursing an angry churning heart for days. You will have peace, even when you don't understand everything.

2. Submission does not always feel natural.

As long as you expect following God to be easy, you will struggle with following God. Just because we are to submit to our husband does not mean that we will automatically *want* to submit. And that's why many of us are saddled with young marriage blues - because we thought we'd never struggle with God's instructions. And because doing marriage God's way doesn't fit like a hand in a glove, we start wondering whether there's something wrong with us. Or God. Or our husband.

I really believe that God wires us up for our destinies – He gives us a passion and disposition to match our calling in life. He has wired us wives to desire headship - security, cover, love and everything that speaks of Christ-like headship.

But something happened in the garden when Eve ate of the fruit and shared it with her husband Adam. Sin entered our lives. And while our spirits have been redeemed through the death and resurrection of Jesus Christ, our flesh is not yet redeemed. It's still in rebellion towards the things of God. It doesn't want to do what our spirit wants to do. Romans 7:14- 15

We have wounds and baggage from the past - people that hurt you, circumstances that broke you. Trust doesn't come easily, and you want people to "prove" themselves before you yield. Your sweet husband, of course, just proved himself unworthy the moment he did that aggravating thing.

Submission is not an automatic switch you flip and it suddenly comes on you! It's more like a journey, something you learn intentionally, and sometimes have to battle through. To win this battle over your flesh, stop expecting easy. God does not take pleasure in our struggles or challenges. Like a good Father, He delights to give us good gifts (Matthew 7:11). But alongside good things, He is interested in our growth and holiness more than our happiness.

So when your personality and the baggage from the past collide to make a big mess in your marriage, it's not the time to quit. It's the time to press through it and insist on what God has promised you; victory.

When God began to teach me real submission, I expected a complete personality makeover. I am not the mildest person I know, I like debates and poking holes in people's opinions. Strong, argumentative and willful didn't seem like good credentials of a submissive wife, so I prayed and asked God to make me a different person. A nicer, milder, sweeter person.

I worked on being sweet, mild and nice. And silently wondered why it was taking long for the new personality to fall on me. I am pretty sure I would have waited for ever hadn't God told me that He wasn't planning on giving me a personality transplant. Rather He was going to transform my heart. Right where I was.

Looking back on these six years, I can say that I have been transformed. The base girl still exists - God didn't inject a new personality. But He renewed and transformed my heart. I am slower to speak, I don't have to have the last word, my husband doesn't have to agree with me on everything. All these, not because God changed my personality but because he transformed my heart. And He's still transforming me.

How about you, how about allowing God to start the process of transformation in your heart? Stop trying to look for shortcuts. You are not your pastor's wife or all the other sweet women you know. (Or you might be the sweet wife who needs to step up) .

Don't sit there, feeling hopeless and helpless, because you failed today. If you mess up, pick yourself up and purpose to do a better job tomorrow. Replaying your dumb words to your husband over again will not make you more submissive. If anything, they'll paralyze you and keep you angry and frustrated. Press into health instead, seeking God. He knows how He wired you, he knows all your issues and wounds. And only He can heal you, not your husband. Don't take it out on him. All you owe him is love! Find your healing in God.

3. Submission doesn't mean you must trust your husband first
We come into marriage believing in reciprocal love; we do our part, he does his. He does a great job as the leader and we trust him as a result. And as long as the dance lasts, marriage is awesome.

And then he overspends on the budget. He stops being as passionate and effusive. He's lackluster on spiritual matters. We begin to look at his performance score sheet and we feel cheated and frustrated. And we think it's insane to submit when he's not delivering a "trustworthy" performance.

Here's something we forget; God's mandate for husbands to lead has nothing to do with their stellar abilities and everything to do with His divine plan. The Bible doesn't say

"For the husband *who is perfect* is head of the wife". It says " For the husband is head of the wife". Period

So as a wife, you are in deep trouble when you lift your eyes from the eternal and get fixated on the temporal. Many times, obedience requires bypassing our carnal inclinations and thoughts. Understanding is not a prerequisite for obedience!

Take another look at Ephesians 5:22: Wives, submit to your own husbands, *as to the Lord.*

See the bigger picture here. It's not your husband, it's the Lord. Come to that place where you release yourself to God and trust His plan for your life. Lasting bliss cannot be crafted any other way but through intentional obedience to *God's plan.* Submission is not your husband's plan, its God's plan.

Don't hold the "trust card" against the "submission card". Don't wait for your husband to "prove" himself before you submit. Husbands are normal human beings, they will make mistakes. They will fail and generally do things that scream "not worthy of trust!".

You know, the same way you do things that scream "not worthy of love!"

Choose to see God, not just man. See the God of your husband. Author Jennifer Smith says "Faith is seeing your husband the way God sees him". To this I add, it's also *acting* in a manner that communicates that faith.

Please note: the kind of trust I am talking about here is the healthy every day trust needed for your marriage to thrive. I am not talking about putting yourself in harm's way in the name of trusting your husband. God does not ask you to submit to abuse or sin. If you find yourself in a harmful situation in marriage, seek help. Don't enable sin or abuse by staying silent.

4. Submission does not mean the absence of a will
One of my issues with submission and the reason I was waiting for God to give me a personality transplant was because I believed true submission meant not having a will.

I thought that wives who had learned to submit had learned to kill their wills. Or perhaps, they never had a will to begin with. But I had a will, strong opinions and feelings on just about every topic and issue. I didn't know what I was supposed to do with my thoughts and opinions.

I have learned that all wives have wills. After all, we are the helpmeets! We have tons of ideas on how to do life and marriage. God brought me up to speed and told me that submission does not mean the absence of a will, but the *yielding* of the will.

It would not be called submission if there was nothing to be submitted, nothing to be yielded.

Strong's Hebrew and Greek Dictionary defines submission as it appears in Ephesians as *hoop-ot-as'-so* which means "to subdue unto" "to subordinate." That means that you do have thoughts and opinions and passions and intelligence, but willingly yield them and prefer another.

Think about it this way; God did not give us an appetite so we could eat anything we want. Along with an appetite, He gave us a mind and self control so we know the right things to eat and when to stop eating.

In the same manner, God does not give us a will so we can dominate and have our way. But with my will and passions and thoughts and emotions, He gave me the ability to grow in discipline and maturity and to know when I am doing my job as the *ezer kenegdo* and when I am pushing for power and control.

It's not that you don't have a say in your marriage, you do. But you don't try to control or manipulate and be on top of every single situation and decision. You trust.

In the same breath, strong marriages are made of two spouses who are pulling together in the same direction. We'll look at this in detail shortly, but I need to reiterate that your thoughts and contributions are important and needed in your marriage.

As a couple, you will see things differently and that's a plus, not a negative. So please hear what I am saying; God gave you that man because it was not good for him to be alone. He needs you. You have a strong role to play in your marriage and you carry it out through cultivating a confident, pliable, trusting heart.

5. Submission won't be demanded of you

I grew up with a tough dad but I married a gentle, easier man. A few months married, I discovered I was so used to being told what to do that when it wasn't demanded of me or spelled out in black and white, I excused myself out of responsibilities.

My husband does not demand submission. And most godly husbands don't walk around waving a "I am the head honcho" placard, demanding acquiescence.

And so wives with gentler husbands can get away with things because "he doesn't mind" or "he doesn't care about things like that."

It becomes easy to get home at whatever time you want because he doesn't fuss about it, while in fact the truth is, he stopped asking about it the third time you waddled in later than committed. That might seem like an unimportant detail, but these small things reveal your attitude about submission.

If staying out late with your girlfriends instead of being home being with your man is ranking higher in your priorities, you have a problem. As long as something is sucking life and oneness out of your relationship, it's selfish and needs to go.

As a wife, quit expecting your husband to keep your heart in order for you. Follow the leading of the Lord. When He convicts you about certain habits and behaviors, leave the thing already. Don't look for cracks in your relationship, small areas you can manipulate and take advantage of. Instead, purpose to be the kind of wife who goes over and above the normal call of duty; of whom it can be said "Her children rise up and call her blessed; Her husband also, and he praises her." Proverbs 31:28

6. Submission is not about a woman's value

We already mentioned this in passing earlier but I feel it's important to talk about it some more.

One of the reasons women struggle with submission in marriage is because they haven't understood who they truly are. They don't know their identity - whose they are and how much He values them.

Like I once did, you may have tied your "who" to your "do." You've swallowed the lie that your worth is tied to your abilities. That unless you are in control of your life - or something - unless you are out there leading, then you are nothing.

We mentioned this earlier; God did not create you to be in charge of your own life.

Author & Bible teacher Beth Moore says "Man has no sovereign authority. We cannot be our own bosses no matter how much we deny our purpose. Yes, God ordains human government and places people in high positions - but always under His divine dominion"[6]

Here's the truth sweet sister of mine, God's love (and ultimately His plan), is not tied to our performance or abilities. He loves and values you just the way you are - with all your issues and pain and wounds. In fact, God loved you before you loved him. He was thinking about you before you thought about Him. He sent His son to die for you before you said "yes" to Him. He doesn't love you more because you go to church or try to love your husband better. There's nothing you can do to deserve God's love or increase/decrease the value He's put on you. It's there and there's nothing you can do about it. The only thing you can do is accept it.

While we (men and women) are assigned differently, we are valued, accepted and loved equally.

7. Submission does not mean you play doormat
Often, when we talk about submission, most wives immediately conjure images of a placid doormat. But submission is not burying your head

in the sand, hoping all marital challenges will go away. It's not keeping quiet when you should be speaking up. It's not enabling unhealthy marriage dynamics in the name of "respecting my husband as the leader." It's not shutting your brain when your input is needed.

Proverbs 27:17 KJV says, "Iron sharpeneth iron; so a man sharpeneth the countenance of his friend."

Your husband and your marriage need you. Pick up your responsibilities, engage, offer constructive feedback on issues.

If one of you is doing something they shouldn't, it's the other person's responsibility to call them out, with respect and love. For example, if your husband asks you to watch porn with him, you shouldn't join him and call that submission. That's joining in his sin.

You have been called to submit to God's will first. (Ephesians 5:21) If your husband's will and the Lord's will collide, you choose the Lord. Being your husband's *ezer kenego* means that you both do some heavy lifting, sharpening one another and encouraging one another in Christ.

Husbands have been commanded to love their wives as Christ loves his church. Christ does not abuse his bride or put her in danger. God so loves and cares for women that husbands who dishonor their wives are hindered in their prayers. (1 Peter 3:7).

8. Submission is not up for redefinition
I find it easy to listen to and support my husband when he's making all the right decisions. And by "right", I mean decisions I agree with. But when we discuss things and he doesn't see my point of view, backing off and allowing him to make that final decision - and supporting him in it – can be challenging sometimes. It's easy for me to redefine submission at that moment.

You may have come into marriage wounded and carrying baggage that makes you believe you cannot fully trust a man. That you always have to 'leave a little bit' of yourself and to look out for yourself. Or maybe your husband has disappointed you and you feel you can't trust his decisions.

Please note, I am not talking about reckless or chronic issues here, such as leaving all the financial decisions to him when he has a history of financial mismanagement and is yet to get whole in that area. For those things, you must exercise caution and wisdom. I am talking about the growth pains that come with doing life with another human being, about the stretching that comes when you become one flesh with your husband.

The Bible says that God's word stands forever (Isaiah 40:8). It's unchanging and His ways are not up for re-editing. And that's just perfect for us because if they were, we'd have edited Him out of our lives all together.

You can't pick and choose what to agree to. It's either all or nothing. In the end, you are either following that man or you are not. You cannot decide how much you follow or for how long or when you will follow or how you will follow. It's either all the way - accepting the whole command from the Lord - or nothing at all.

When we buck against the order of marriage, we buck against God. This is not a good place to be when you are seeking a way out of bluesland!

God, the Author of marriage and your creator, has a plan for you personally, and it includes healing and restoring every part of you that's broken, every inclination to self-preserve. God knows why you opened that secret bank account. He knows why you feel helpless in the bedroom.

Maybe you don't consider yourself broken, just forward thinking and liberated. It's funny how we think that we can be liberated from our roles, isn't it? We think it's possible to veer off from our original purpose. But that's not liberation. It's slavery. You can't liberate a pen from writing. It's a pen, it was made to write. As much as you may not like it, you want your husband to lead. God made you to *want* cover. That's why you are upset when you think he's not doing enough as a leader.

Your answer lies in God. He wants to come into every hurting, painful, even prideful area of your heart. Without His healing you will stay mired in submission blues and that's not His best for you at all.

What To do When Your Husband Will not Lead

You might be reading this and thinking, "You have no idea what's going on in my house, I am not the problem, he is! He doesn't make decisions, he's not responsible with money, he doesn't even care that I am trying to honor and submit to him!"

I hear you, wife. It's one thing to do your part, quite another for your hubby to do his. In my own marriage, I have had moments when I felt like I was doing all that was required of me and my husband wasn't. I have looked heavenward with a furrowed brow and asked, "What's up with this, Lord?" I am my husband has had similar moments.

I will tell you the same thing I have felt the Lord say to me. It's not my responsibility to put my husband's heart in order. That's His job. I get to do some tough-love things yes, like get over myself, reach out to our mentors, bring up hard conversations. But in the end, God is the only one who can change the heart of my husband.

In this book, my desire is to encourage you to do your part in building a strong foundation for your marriage in these early years. That's what we've been working through - how to be well even when our circumstances are less than lovely. I cannot speak for husbands because I am not a man. What I know is that Christ has not called us to do our part only when our life and marriage is good. He's called us to live and reflect His glory all through life, *especially* when our circumstances are less than ideal.

Luke 6:32-36 says, *"But if you love those who love you, what credit is that to you? For even sinners love those who love them. And if you do good to those who do good to you, what credit is that to you? For even sinners do the same. And if you lend to those from whom you hope to receive back, what credit is that to you? For even sinners lend to sinners to receive as much back. But love your enemies, do good, and lend, hoping for nothing in return; and your reward will be great, and you will be sons of the Most High. For He is kind to the unthankful and evil. Therefore be merciful, just as your Father also is merciful."*

As we move on, please understand that God *does want* your husband to take up his leadership responsibility. You are not wrong in desiring these things. God designed marriage to function in a certain way and he desires to see your marriage flying on both wings.

If you're reading this and what you're dealing with is an abusive situation, you need to seek immediate help and intervention. Otherwise, here are some thoughts on what to do if your husband has not fully embraced his leadership role:

1. Understand you cannot change him
I know. Sounds unfair, doesn't it? You are thinking "Really? With all the changes He needs to make in his life and you think I should do nothing?" At least that's how I used to think.

I thought if I tried hard enough, I could change Tommy. He wasn't abdicating his responsibilities per se but he was a brand new husband. He was in over his head, as most newlyweds are. He was learning leadership (as I was learning submission, but funny how we like to extend grace to ourselves but not to our husbands). We had challenges from communication to ministry to money. And I had a specific way of looking at things - in other words I believed I was right. I wasn't keen on seeing things from his angle. The depth of my issue? I had no grace to give. And most newlywed wives don't either, because they are *unlearning* the singular way of thinking and living.

As a sparkling new wife, I took up operation-change-my-husband with gusto. Many months down the line, after a lot of frustration and hurt, I began to respond to the divine tap on my shoulder. God reminded me about my own salvation. That as much as He loved me and desired a relationship with me, so much that He sent His beloved Son to die for me, He didn't force that gift down my throat. I had to make the decision to love Him back through accepting Jesus as my Savior and Lord.

It's called free will.

Much as you'd like your husband to make changes in his life and become more responsible, he will have to make the changes himself, with the help of the Holy Spirit. You can't guilt him, intimidate, manipulate or coerce him to change. Oh, maybe you can nag and fret and quarrel. But that will not give you the bliss you are looking for. In fact, it will take you in the opposite direction, keeping you in the grips of the very blues you are trying to escape.

Here's what you need to do instead - respectfully communicate your heart and the things that are bothering you. Do your part, including the other things we are discussing in this chapter. But do have it settled in your heart that you can't make him be what you want him to be. Even when it's for his own good.

2. Be honest with yourself

As a new bride, I believed my husband needed to be like me. I was a workaholic, people-pleasing extrovert, while Tommy was an easy-going introvert. In no time, it became apparent that he didn't care for my "work ethic," which included over-extending myself and constantly worrying about work and people.

Being Mr Easy, he was unmoved by chaotic programs and people. Being Ms not-easy, I was moved by chaotic people and programs - I am drawn to disorder and power vacuums, and I work hard to bring order. When my husband "lagged" behind - because bulldozing his way is not his style - I worked hard to cover for him. I carried his imagined load and worried myself sick.

Are you there in your marriage right now? Running all over the place trying to cover for your husband where he needs no cover? Busy taking responsibility for areas you have no business taking responsibility? When you think about it, what's the real trigger of all your issues? Is it really your husband or is it just you?

Later I would learn that if I had no prior expectation on my husband to be like me, I would have no problems with his leadership style. His style and my style were, and will always be different, as different as any introvert and extrovert can be. My answer lay, not in sorting out his heart and leadership style, but in changing myself and my expectations. As an introvert, he sure needed to improve on his people skills and self motivation. But even then, any improvements and growth would still be different from me because we were two different people.

If you believe your husband is not doing his part as a leader in your home, I encourage you to stop by your heart first. Examine yourself. Ask yourself the hard questions, "Is something really wrong with him or am I just looking at things with the wrong lenses?" "Am I trying to dictate the kind of relationship he should have with the Lord?" "What have I done/not done that may have influenced this behavior?"

These questions are not to excuse his behavior or to try and shift blame & responsibility, but to help you find areas where you need to work on yourself.

3. Pray and release your husband to God.
Prayer should be on top of the list but I put it here purposely because it's important to have clarity on the first two areas to avoid praying the "change-him-for-me" type of prayers.

When you feel like your husband is not taking his role seriously, it's easy focus on the pain, the inconvenience and frustration of his "irresponsibility" that all you think about is how to make it stop. And it's easy to pray that God would make him change so that *you* can be comfortable.

Obviously, God does not want us to suffer needlessly. But He's not nearly as interested in our comfort and convenience as much as we are.

He's more interested in the condition of our hearts. He wants to change us to be like Him, and He uses the different challenges we go through in life to help us know Him. (Romans 8:28).

The most effective prayer for your husband originates from a place of sincerity and security in God. A place devoid of expectations, where you've released your husband from a long list of "to-be" or "to-do". A place filled with agape love and repentance of your own sin. Yes, *your* sin. Your fear, lack of faith, anger, mumbling, quarreling, ungratefulness. You see, it's easy to see the speck in your husband's eye and miss the big log in your own. But true prayer and intercession for your husband can only begin once you see and repent of the log in your eye. Only then can you be an effective prayer warrior.

James 5:16 NIV says "Therefore confess your sins to each other and pray for each other so that you may be healed. The prayer of a righteous person is powerful and effective."

Your prayer is powerful and effective because it comes from righteous-ness.

This morning I woke up and I couldn't shake off this thought - God wants me to love my husband the way he is. Not the way he will be to-morrow. I realized I have so many expectations on my husband and it's easy to stare into the future and fail to completely embrace and enjoy and cherish what we have now...because I am looking at the distance we need to travel. God reminded me that changing my husband was His job. Loving my husband, right where he is, is my job.

Will you embrace your job with me? Will you pray for your husband and allow God to work in him? The beautiful thing about prayer is that it changes us first. I love this divine plan of God, that as we draw near to him in fellowship and prayer, He begins to flood our hearts with a peace that defies our circumstances and challenges. It blesses me that I don't have to wait for my husband to be a certain way before I can experience the joy of the Lord in our marriage!

4. Purpose to go the extra mile

Last week I was reading the story of Lazarus in John 11. I was struck by verse 40 which says,

"Jesus said to her (Martha), "Did I not say to you that if you would believe you would see the glory of God?" (Brackets added)

At that point, Martha was trying to reason Jesus out of opening the tomb. After all, Lazarus had been dead four days and there was surely a stink.

But when we look back to verse 23, Jesus had told Martha that her brother would rise again.

Martha had forgotten Jesus' promise because the situation was dire.

Is your husband's "abdication" looking like a dead case today? Or do you believe he can change and become the leader that God created him to be? Like Martha, it's not easy to believe that dead-looking situations can come back to life. Because death - the struggle and challenge, his inability or unwillingness to pick up his responsibility - feels so real and painful and acute.

Nonetheless, and in order to see the glory of God in your marriage, you have to ignore what your eyes and mind see and cling to the word of the Lord. You will have to act and think and talk based off His word to you, not based on what you see.

That means going the extra mile in your marriage, loving sacrificially, submitting and honoring him as your head, even when you think he's not doing a good job of it. (Note: Again, I am not talking about submitting yourself to sin or abuse)

Remember that no man comes into marriage having figured out the ways of a husband. He learns as he goes. Sometimes, the responsibility is overwhelming. As his wife, your job is not to make his life more difficult by constantly pointing out areas he's failing at. Instead come alongside, be his partner. Encourage him, thank him for what he does well already (don't give me the side eye, you married the man, surely he did one thing right?). Lower your expectations and understand that he is growing, as you are. Don't complain and murmur as you do these things, do it as unto the Lord!

5. Even with outside help, remember you still have to work it out
When we were working out our early marriage kinks, we had meetings with our mentors. We sat down for coffee, met in their homes and offices to chat. Then we'd head home... and two days later I'd have something fresh to be upset about.

In my mind, getting counseling meant having immediate answers. I wanted to see changes, or at least something that indicated change. I think most of us are like that, planting a seed today and expecting a bumper harvest by evening.

But just because you talked with a counselor or mentor does not mean everything has been straightened out!

When working through the leadership kink, don't be rush, expecting immediate results. Don't relax and wash your hands off your faith and belief because someone told your husband what he needs to do. You must stay engaged!

Counseling marks the beginning of hard work, not the end. You still have to go back home and continue to submit and love and pray and go the extra mile and do all those things you need to do. The purpose of counseling is to offer you a fresh perspective and encouragement (and a kick in your hind). You still have to go home and *walk out* issues.

6. Continue to do your part and appreciate small steps
Here's where the rubber meets the road. You can't stop submitting because he's not leading or loving you the way Christ instructs him to. Just because he's not doing his part does not excuse you from doing yours.

I know it's difficult to submit when you feel your husband is unloving or not taking his responsibility seriously. You want to make all the decisions, ignore his input, take the reins and run.

But that won't usher the bliss you are looking for.

Nowhere in the Bible does God promise easy obedience. On the contrary Jesus says "If anyone desires to come after Me, he must deny himself, and take up his cross and follow Me." Matthew 16:24.

When you feel like you have the short end of the stick, practice gratitude and seeing Who you are ultimately submitting to. Take your eyes off man and see the Author of your marriage. The One who has a good plan for your life and marriage, no matter what happens along the way. Nothing catches God by surprise; nothing is out of His control. God can and will use your faithfulness in difficult times to win the heart of your husband. (1 Peter 3:1-2)

Purpose to be the kind of person who sees other areas of marriage that are working. Don't allow yourself to be so tunnel-visioned that you forget the other blessings of God in your life. Count your blessings and focus on what your husband is, not what he isn't. He might not be telling you he loves you as much as you like, he might not be helping you out as much as you want, he might not even be as "spiritual" as you are. But does he come home to you every night, is he faithful to you, does he still love God? Focus and build on that.

Purpose to notice the areas he's improving on. Appreciate him and thank him when he does something he normally doesn't do. Don't fixate on the next area he needs to start working on. And don't get exasperated when there are setbacks in his journey. Appreciating his efforts will encourages him to try again.

Go on and celebrate the areas of your marriage that are working and as you do, your joy will be a testament to your husband. Nobody likes the company of a wet blanket or a chronic complainer, but everyone loves the positive sunny-side up type of person. Purpose to see the sunny side of your marriage. Because, believe me, God's grace is there, even when you think it's not.

Now, I am not saying that God will answer your prayer if you do these things, or that your husband will change if you follow steps 1-2-3. Not really. There are never guarantees but we have a higher chance of experiencing growth and transformation when we become all that God called us to be, in spite of our circumstances.

7. Don't quit.
I was talking with someone the other day and she was feeling particularly hopeless about a certain situation in her marriage. The situation had moved from bad to worse over a couple of months and she was feeling like giving up.

As I encouraged her, I remembered my own struggle five years ago when things were not so rosy in certain parts. I had tried all I knew and things were not improving. I told my mentor that I was going to quit trying and just let things be. My mentor responded "Don't quit!" He said it with such fierceness and fire and down the road, I see what he meant.

Quitting is not a neutral action. When you give up hope, you don't stay at that same spot. You move backward. There's no neutrality with hope, you either have it or you don't. You are either moving forward in hope and faith, or moving backward in despair.

Someone has to be rooting for the health of your marriage. And if you think your husband is not rooting for the health of your marriage, who else is left but you? You and God are a majority.

Consider this; what if God has allowed you to come to the end of your rope and wits, so that you can let go and allow Him to do the work? You see, sometimes we are so deep in our blues we don't even realize how much we've put our faith in other things other than God. As earlyweds, there's so much to learn about the workings of a marriage - we don't know where we end and where God begins. We hear, read and see all kinds of advice and we rush home to apply it. Many times, without knowing it, we begin to put our hopes in formulas and principles more than God, the Source of all life.

Sometimes, we need to max out our strength so we can turn to God's strength. God has deep mysteries to show us about marriage and often we learn them through hard times and trials.

If it looks as though your husband will never lead or love you the way Christ wants, I want you to understand that God has not run out of grace. Isaiah 54;5 says "your maker is your husband". God will fill you and meet your needs. Your part is to keep hope in Him alive.

8. Watch your AWA
AWA is an acronym I use for Attitude, Words and Actions.

Let's start with your Words
Women are natural word-slingers. When hurt or disappointed, we turn our words into lethal missiles that obliterate everything in our path. We think that our words are a "mirror of reality" or that they will "motivate" a husband to change. The truth is, men don't get motivated by verbal beat-downs. In fact, nobody does.

Proverbs 18:21 warns us that death and life are in the power of the tongue, and those who love it will eat its fruits.

Do you want life or death in your marriage? Do you want your husband to rise up and be the leader God created Him to be? Then let all your words align with that belief! Don't go calling him what he's not and expect him to surprise you. (Read that again and let it to sink in).

Negative words not only affect your husband, they also affect you. They affirm, fortify and amplify what you see. God's word, on the other hand, is truth and life! Everything (your marriage blues included) that doesn't align to God's promise and truth is a lie!

So speak God's word, not your pain, anger and disappointment. When you choose God's perspective over "reality," your words become an instrument of change, unleashing the power of God to work in your man's heart and life.

Your Attitude

Your husband doesn't need words to know exactly what you think about him. What goes on in your heart in secret oozes out through your attitude. Attitude is like an invisible blanket, a silent code that transmits your true beliefs. Sometimes you aren't even aware of the transmission, but it's clearly discernible to those closest to you.

You have to do more than just "train" your mouth *not* to say the wrong thing. You have to train your heart to dwell on the right thing, so that eventually your mouth speaks the right thing.

We find the right thing in the fourth chapter of Paul's epistle to the Philippians:

"Finally, brethren, whatever things are true, whatever things are noble, whatever things are just, whatever things are pure, whatever things are lovely, whatever things are of good report, if there is any virtue and if there is anything praiseworthy—meditate on these things."

Focus on changing from the inside-out, not merely behavior modification. Surface changes can bring temporary relief but they don't bring lasting change. You can only act a certain way for so long or withhold your words for so long. Your true self will rear its head after a while. But a heart that is being transformed and changed is steady, and is ultimately, the only way for permanent change.

Your Actions

The story is told of a wife who carried the weight in her marriage for a long time. Her husband was slacking in his responsibilities and she had been covering for him. One day and desperate for change, she decided not to pay the house rent. Soon the landlord came by and locked the family out of their house. Her husband was shocked and shamed by the lock-out and quickly began to pick up his responsibilities.

Now, you might read that and start thinking of all the ways you can get your husband to do his job! Hold your horses and listen to the heart behind the story. Stepping-back in your actions is not a means to shame, control or manipulate your husband to do something. When you think about the wife in this story, she suffered and got embarrassed right alongside her husband. But she realized that she'd never given her words and attitudes any legs – she had been an enabling his behavior by taking up his responsibilities. When she finally gave her words some legs, she paid the price right along her husband.

Sometimes we fear letting go of the reins even when holding on is hurting us instead of helping us. We want a strong man but we still want to stay in charge. Unfortunately, you can't have your cake and eat it. If you want your husband to lead, you need to get out of his way. Like this lady, it might mean going through seasons of hardships and adjustments. It all depends on how badly you want God to move in your marriage.

Bottom line; as you adjust your actions to match your heart and words, your real goal is to leave the scene so that God can work.

Wrapping Up

"Submission and authority function hand-in-hand with all the other biblical directives about how Christians ought to interact with one another. Along with submitting to her husband, a Christian wife also has the responsibility to be transparent, speak truth, confront sin, and challenge her husband to ever increasing levels of holiness. As heirs together of the grace of life, both husband and wife have the responsibility to love, encourage, and build one another up; and to interact with forbearance, kindness and humility. Biblical authority and submission contribute to mutuality, and do not diminish or detract from it."[7]

5

Loving the choice you made; how to build a hedge around your love.

Being 'one flesh' in marriage means that the relationship is not the source of security, affirmation, control, or value. Those issues of identity need to be rooted in Christ

-Scott Perkins

"Therefore shall a man leave his father and his mother, and shall cleave unto his wife: and they shall be one flesh" Genesis 2:24 KJV

From the passage above, you first leave your parents before you cleave and become one flesh with your spouse. Most of us understand leaving our "father and mother". But we don't understand that "leaving" includes departing our former ways and lifestyle of singlehood.

I learned the lesson very quickly in my early days.

A few weeks after our wedding, my church cell group (small group) was hosting an afternoon party and my husband and I were invited. We were just resuming normal church activities after a brief honeymoon hiatus. Because we were from a large church, my husband and I had different pastors and cell groups. At the point of resuming church activities, we were still in transition, still trying to figure out which cell group we would settle in to as a couple.

Personally, I had been part of my cell group for years and I was looking forward to getting back to "normal". And introducing my husband! On the day of the party, which was a Sunday afternoon, and right after the morning church service, my husband mentioned, quite casually, that he did not feel like going to the party. I thought he was joking. But quickly discovered he was not.

"Really? You don't feel like going?" I was confused. But we had given our word!

"Yeah, I really don't. But you can go" He was trying to ease my worry but instead managed to drive it right through the roof.

The highlight of the party, for me at least, was getting to introduce him to everyone! And what new bride goes to Couple functions alone!

My anger quickly turned cold. *What in the world am I going to tell my pastor, what will they think of us, of me, of my choice for a husband!*

And then it was downhill from there.

What did his refusal to attend fellowship mean, was that a sign of his disinterest in God? Was our marriage doomed? All we had was God and if my husband didn't like God that much, how would we survive? And we were barely out of our honeymoon, what other terrible discoveries lay ahead?

Eventually I would inform my mentor about our no-show. And my wise spiritual mum told me "go home and make him the best lunch ever". (Oh but the last thing I was planning to do was make him any sort of lunch!)

That was my first day of "Cleaving101" - learning what it means to leave the old ways, associations, family and lifestyles and beginning to cleave to the one I had vowed my life to.

It turned out that leaving some parts of singlehood - a cold bed, a silent house, zero man presence e.t.c is easy. Cleaving to the nice part of marriage - a warm bed, a hunky man, a shoulder to cry on e.t.c equally easy.

But when cleaving begins to demand separation from old friendships and creation of new boundaries and allegiances, the difficulties roar in.

(In case you are still wondering, my husband was struggling with the whole "in-law" thing - that's what my spiritual parents and sisters and brothers were to him. He needed some space to figure out his place. And being an introvert, he also wanted a *quiet* weekend with his wife.)

If no one tells us, as earlyweds, that leaving and cleaving can be all shades of difficult, we will make our bed in blues land.

Strong's Concordance renders "Leaving" as it appears in the verse Genesis 2:24 as "to abandon, forsake, neglect, let loose, set free, let go."

Cleaving means "to cling, stay close, stick to, follow closely"

These are *doing* phrases; they involve action. Uncomfortable-sounding action, I might add. They are doing words, they involve movement.

What does that mean for us? It means that leaving and cleaving is something we get to do for ourselves, with the help of God. It cannot be done on our behalf. Much as you want to blame your mum for interfering in your marriage, the responsibility for drawing boundaries lies with you.

Leaving Your Past Behind

In his book The Purpose and Power of Love and Marriage, the late Dr Myles Munroe has this to say about Genesis 2:24

"One flesh does not simply mean gluing of two people together but rather the "fusion' of two distinct elements into one. If I glue two pieces of wood together, they are bonded but not fused. ..when two elements are fused together they become inseparable."

For these two elements to fuse together there must be a purity within the elements. Impurity within the elements would interfere with the quality and strength of adhesion. When two become one, there must be a purity within and between them. They must let go of everything that might interfere with the quality and strength of their union. Old mindsets, singular thinking, hurts and wounds have to be left behind in order to fuse and cleave properly.

Marriage and leadership coaches (and our mentors) Barnabas and Grace Achoki, put it this way "The two cannot be one as long as one is still holding on to Mama. Two is company and three is definitely a crowd in marriage."

Cleaving is not a Quick or Automatic Process

Sometime back I was talking to a bride-to-be who was days away from her wedding. I can't recall our exact words but I remember her response to something I said: "Hey people say that honeymoon ends, but that's not the truth. Honeymoon doesn't have to end."

She was spot on of course. But I knew she would soon find out that lasting honeymoon is cultivated, not automatic. So I explained that for marriage to thrive and have extended honeymoon, she will have to do some *intentional* work.

We can't fold our hands and expect love to thrive unattended.

You see, it's easy to glue together when everything is working as it should, what I call the unintentional honeymoon. When both of you have your best foot forward, you can follow each other to the moon and back.

But then at some point you will meet his real human side; water running as he brushes his teeth, clothes on the floor, helping a total of zero times when both of you have had a long day. He will meet *your* human side; monthly hormonal mood swings, tendency to talk on the phone forever, a penchant for shopping and a wonderful "gift" of seeing all that's wrong with him.

It's at that time that you will have to *choose* to cleave. Not because you feel like it, not because it feels "fair," but because you vowed "for better or for worse."

If you are waiting for an easy, automatic cleave switch, it doesn't exist. It's a life-long endeavor where you discover new ways to choose your spouse in changing times. It's a learning process that involves intentional choices and grace-infused giving.

How Familiarity Dulls the Cleaving Process

Ladies, isn't it easy to put on a stellar show during courtship?

Remember all the effort you put into getting ready for a date with your guy? Your make-up, clothes, shoes and accessories were carefully chosen. You went all out to look good. When you sat in that café and conversed, you didn't let it all hang out. Your words, I mean. You measured them, you were careful with what you said and how you said it. You hang onto his every word. You admired him, made him feel like a hero, just for being who he was. He didn't have to take out the trash, didn't have to have all his ducks in a row. He was loved just for showing up!

Then you got married, and you settled into your *post-date* routine. Remember how after every awesome date, you went back home and washed off the make-up, kicked off the high heels, slipped into comfy house wear and generally nestled back to your normal real self?

Until the next date.

Now marriage has become one long *post-date* routine. We have nestled into our "real" selves and routines. We don't put much effort towards our looks or behavior. Now we want him to earn that love, deserve that praise and sweetness and respect we lavished for free before marriage. Showing up, just being there, is no longer enough.

Before you start throwing tomatoes my way, believe me, I know life has changed. It's hard to pull off courtship life in marriage. You can't be in high heels and full make-up and great hair all day long, every day.

The point I am trying to make here is that the very things that drew you to one another, the things that made you interesting to each other, the small things that captivated you are the very things that keep your marriage exciting and fresh. In fact, to get your marriage roaring, not just sizzling, you must continue to discover and add more things to your armory of love.

So while you might not be able to wear that knock out dress he likes throughout the day, you don't have to look like something the cat dragged in either. You can comb your hair, wear clothes that show form, smell nice, be well-groomed and brush your teeth. Apply something on your lips, even if it's just plain Vaseline, so your lips are soft and kiss-able. Do something to stay appealing! You don't have to buy expensive clothes. As a start, think about what you are putting on, the colors, the combinations, the fit. Look at yourself in the mirror and ask yourself, would I love to come home to that, would I be attracted to that? I know as women we are not typically visual by nature, but our men are!

Marriage is not your ticket to frumpy-land!

As I type this, it's a very cold wintry afternoon and I am nestled in thick gray pants and an even thicker brown jacket! I am a very practical person and I tend to go for function and comfort, over girly-girl things. My husband is the opposite, he will pick beauty over function, as far as my wardrobe is concerned. I have to be intentional about what I wear - especially during winter months! – because I can be *overly* functional and forget beauty or style.

Something else you need to understand; taking care of yourself is not just for the benefit of your honey. It's for your benefit as well. At the time of writing this book, I work from home. That means I don't go out and meet people every day. I don't have to dress up for the outside world. And thus it's really easy to let go and be all humdrum. Guess who shows up for my frumpy party? Confidence issues. The head and heart begin to take cues from how I treat my body.

So I have to be intentional about how I look. And so do you. Don't allow the downward spiral, step up your game.

Remember your home is your resting place, your oasis, your ministry, where the rest of your life springs from. You need to take care of yourself while there. Make your life beautiful from home and your beauty shall nourish the rest of your life and the people around you.

He Needs Your Admiration

My husband and I live in America but we are from Kenya. The months leading up to our relocation three and a half years ago were long and stress-filled. My husband was working long, hard hours, preparing to launch a flagship product at work. At that point, his career had peaked and he was receiving a lot of recognition and accolades.

On the other hand, preparing to relocate was a rigorous process, filled with paperwork and mandatory processes. Since my husband was busy, working out the many details of our move fell on me. It was a heavy load and over time I became resentful and frustrated. I don't need to tell you that I was least-enthused about his work achievements and progress. All I could see was what he hadn't done and how he wasn't there for me. He on the other hand was dying for some admiration and respect.

A man can receive all the celebration and admiration the world has to offer but what matters to him is the celebration and admiration he gets from his wife. I would learn that the hard way.

Men thrive on respect. During challenging times, they want to know they are respected *inspite* of their "performance". My husband knew that he was letting me down, but he didn't need to be reminded about it all the time. (Plus, he was doing the best he could at that point). What he desired was a wife who noticed and acknowledged the other good things he was doing instead of camping on what was not happening.

Sure we both could have done a better job in helping each other out. But at the end of the day, someone has to break the cycle. Someone has to make the choice to get out of the ride to blues-land. That someone *could* have been me - listening, noticing and admiring him, doing my part (and his too, where I could) and trusting God for wisdom and energy to do what needed to be done.

My point here is to help us understand the intentionality of marriage. We cultivate oneness, not just when our circumstances are ideal, but also when they are not.

We put ourselves in our spouse's shoes and walk a mile. Matthew 7: 12 MSG says, "Here is a simple, rule-of-thumb guide for behavior: Ask yourself what you want people to do for you, then grab the initiative and do it for them."

He Needs Your Respect More than Your Love

As women we tend to give our husbands what *we* like the most. Since we are wired for love, we assume our husbands crave love the most, and we smoother them with affection. But truth is, most men would rather be respected than loved. I can't say I understand how that works because I am a girl: give me some love, any day every day, baby!

But I don't have to understand how it works to bless my husband! To grow in oneness, figure out the different ways you can give him the one thing that makes him happy; respect. Be proactive, making intentional choices that speak "I respect you".

Since no two men are the same, you might want to ask questions like "What communicates respect to you the most?" or "What do I do (or not do) that communicates respect to you?"

Hopefully, you'll get an answer but even if you don't get a straight answer the first time round, the fact that you are thinking about it communicates something to him. Whether you ask the questions or not, here are a few things that generally communicate respect to men:

- Noticing, admiring and appreciating his hard work and advancement at work.
- Admiring the different and unique ways he contributes in your home. For example, my husband makes a mean vegetable-fruit-nut salad! I love to talk about it when we have guests over. You don't have to wait for an audience, of course. Let him know how much you appreciate what he does at home.
- Initiating sex, and enjoying it!
- Admiring his gifts and abilities, the things that set him apart from other people.

The list can go on. Please find a recommended resource at the end of this book on this subject.[1]

He Needs Your Attention

We've talked about that adoring attention you gave him when you were courting. Do you know that when he married you, he believed he was going to get more of it, not less?!

If your husband was a treasure before the wedding, he is now an even bigger treasure in marriage. Vows were taken, a covenant was made before God and man. The stakes are higher.

But a treasure which is neglected will begin to lose its luster. The loss though, does not begin in our actions - like becoming less attentive to the little details of marriage that mean the world to him. It begins in our minds, when other things begin to rank higher than the man we vowed our lives to.

Don't starve him of your attention. When he gets home in the evening, stop whatever you are doing; acknowledge him, kiss him, hug him. When he's talking to you, turn towards him and give him your attention. Prioritize your couple time; be present when you are together.

I am what you can call a high level multi-tasker and I struggle with doing one thing at a time. I thrive when there's variety! While I have purposed to end my work day when my husband walks through the door from work, it's not easy to shut it all out. Often, my gadgets are still blinking and beckoning to do one more thing - check email, share one more article on Pinterest, write down thoughts, network with another blogger, fold the laundry, read something. All this while, I am supposed to be bonding and hanging out with my husband.

I am a work in progress. And so are most of us. The key is to be aware of all those things that are trying to steal your attention. Shut them out and refocus.

You must Create and Observe Boundaries to Protect Your Oneness in Marriage

Awhile back I talked about boundaries in marriage on my marriage blog IntentionalToday.com. The articles raised quite a raucous. Opinions flew like old papers in the storm: "We trust one another!" "We are not kids." "Nothing can happen!" "That's just juvenile and ridiculous!" "We are not in the fifties."

Many people don't see what lasting bliss and regulating our behavior have in common.

I have discovered that people who dislike the idea of boundaries in marriage have not experienced the repercussions of broken trust and relationships. Or if they have, they haven't accepted how such actions played a part.

In Ephesians 5:1-4 ESV Paul says

"Therefore be imitators of God, as beloved children. And walk in love, as Christ loved us and gave himself up for us, a fragrant offering and sacrifice to God. But sexual immorality and all impurity or covetousness must not even be named among you, as is proper among saints. Let there be no filthiness nor foolish talk nor crude joking, which are out of place, but instead let there be thanksgiving."

Look at the first part of that Scripture. Paul asks us to be imitators of God. How do we imitate God? By walking in love. How did God reveal His love to us? By sending His son to die on the cross for us. So what is Paul is asking us to do? He's asking us to take up our cross and follow Jesus. That means sacrifice and a willingness to do what it takes to be like Jesus.

In other words, a lasting happily-ever-after will not be found in doing everything we want, but in doing everything Christ commands.

Marriage does not make us immune to temptation and wandering. If anything it makes us more vulnerable. Because the moment we commit ourselves to something, tests will come.

Remember the last time you committed to something, say a healthier diet? Think about it. Didn't everyone in the office suddenly decide to eat the greasiest, most wonderful-smelling burgers and fries *every* single day?

The enemy of marriage hates marriage and everything that God loves. Once you commit to doing marriage God's way, he'll begin to show up in areas you least expected.

So here's the question to ask yourself: *Is your marriage a treasure? Does it deserve your highest attention and care?*

No one stores valuable treasures in open unsafe places. Instead, we store them in safe secure environments – away from thieves or perilous conditions. Consider this; you can have all sorts of security devices installed in your home but unless you lock your front door, those devices are useless.

In other words, all the trust and love in the world won't help your marriage if you don't take care of the basics. Thinking that "love is enough", or "we trust each other", without basic precautions, is an open door.

Keeping Boundaries with the Opposite Sex

When I hear wives fuss about boundaries with the opposite sex, two questions come to mind; "Why did you get married in the first place? Didn't you understand the basic concept of exclusivity?"

I am not suggesting unmarried people don't have boundaries. But I am saying that once married, we must "up" our boundaries, not relax them. The stakes are higher because we are now spoken for!

We'll look at the details shortly but there's something we must understand; many people who've had extramarital affairs say they did not go looking for one.

It somehow happened. How? Slowly. One boundary broken over time. A stranger allowed into the sacred space reserved for a spouse. A small leak that gives way to a mighty flood.

I am not saying we cannot relate to the opposite sex after marriage. We can but not in the same way we did before marriage.

Before I give you some best practices for boundaries in marriage, let's be clear about what I am *not* saying. I am not saying that you will jump into bed with any guy because you had lunch with them. Or you should become a hermit and avoid all contact with the opposite sex.

No. Building a hedge around your love is about honoring, preferring and pouring yourself into your marriage that everything else becomes secondary. You cut out distractions and anything that might dishonor or create confusion.

With that out of the way, here are a few best practices for boundaries with the opposite sex.

1. Be intentional about your exes
That old boyfriend? Let them go. Delete their phone numbers, don't chat with them online. Don't go looking for and "friending" them on Facebook or other social media.

You can't cleave to your husband when your eyes are looking backward. You must die to that past and focus on being one with the person God gave you.

2. Draw clear physical boundaries
Don't go out alone with persons of the opposite sex. Don't make a habit of giving them rides alone in your car. Don't counsel someone of the opposite sex alone; bring your husband along if you have to counsel or refer the person to another person of their gender. If you must counsel or hold meetings with the opposite sex, keep the office door open or

talk in large open spaces, within sight of others.

That might sound harsh, even ridiculous. But cleaving and protecting the unity of marriage is a counter-cultural, counter-flesh endeavor.

1 Timothy 3:2 instructs us to live above reproach. It's not just about what you know as truth i.e. this is my colleague or he is just a friend. It's also about what others perceive as truth.

Loren Pinilis, a time-management and stewardship expert has this to say about boundaries with the opposite sex: "It's not just about protecting your marriage from infidelity – it's also about protecting your reputation from the possibility of infidelity"[2]

3. Set internal boundaries.

Beth Steffaniak, a marriage and life coach also points out "We need to have internal boundaries about how much we allow ourselves to "think" of some opposite sex person in our lives. That "space" is reserved for and committed to our husbands."[3]

External boundaries are a reflection of our internal boundaries. We get in trouble when we continually breach internal boundaries and hope it won't matter. But it does. When you are comparing your husband's listening abilities to that of Patient Peter at work or how special Peter makes you feel, that's not harmless!

Romans 13:14 ESV warns us to "...put on the Lord Jesus Christ, and make no provision for the flesh, to gratify its desires."

4. Talk about your husband when talking to others

Author and speaker Michael Hyatt calls this the best adultery repellent.[4]

I once had a gentleman strike up conversation as we queued at a FedEx office. Typically, people ask me about Africa (must be the dreadlocks) and this day was no different. After being served at the counter and getting what I needed, I made my way to the computer station at the back of the store. Before long, I looked up and saw the gentleman making his way towards my desk.

It turned out he thought I was single, at least that's what I thought from the new direction of his conversation. I quickly cleared the air; he got the point and left quickly. I would have saved us both the awkwardness if I had "name- dropped" my husband earlier!

Don't assume that people will see your ring and know you are off the market. Be intentional. Build yourself up by talking about him. *Warm your cockles,* as my husband would say. And of course in talking about your husband, make sure you are talking about him in a positive, loving manner! Complaining, negative talk or even testy 'jokes' directed at your absent man will open the very doors, not close them.

5. Don't flirt with anyone other than your husband
Flirting outside marriage shouldn't be something that has to be explained in Christian marriage circles. Because it should be obvious that saying "I do" to your husband meant you said "I don't" to other men!

The online dictionary defines flirting as "to act amorously without serious intentions; to play at love"

The only person you should be amorous with, or play at love is your husband. If you respect yourself, your husband and your one-flesh journey, you will pour honor where honor is due. You won't be starting or stoking fires outside your one-flesh union.

Galatians 5 lists some of the works of the flesh and includes sexual immorality, impurity and sensuality. The author goes on to say that "those who practice such things will not inherit the kingdom of God."

What if you're just complimenting them? Well, there's a heaven and earth difference between a simple compliment and flirting. Flirting has sexual undertones. It's an amorous dance devoid of purity.

A compliment is just that - brief, honest and without gray areas. As women, we know when we are giving or receiving a "come-hither" vibe. You can tell when you are encouraging or enjoying flirting with another man.

6. Nurture and protect your connection

My husband and I like to keep each other in the loop about our daily goings on. He works outside the home while I work from home. Many times when he gets home he will mention some of his social conversations with female colleagues. Not everything and not every day, but some things, some days. Once when he had a female barber, he'd come home and tell me what they talked about as she worked on his hair.

I tell him about my day conversations, the emails, phone calls and interactions. We talk about what online events to attend when they are being hosted by a guy. Sometimes I will forward him emails just to keep him in the loop about certain online conversations with the opposite sex.

Our actions might amaze some people but Tommy and I take our marriage vows seriously. We respect and honor one another and we like to nurture transparency and trust.

Our conversations are not forced. They flow naturally out of our friendship and a desire to be one and protect our unity. It's what happens when you polish your treasure. It becomes more valuable and you find yourself wanting to keep it safe.

This is not to say that you should now go to your husband and demand that he details all the conversations he's had with women. It doesn't work that way! If openness and accountability is an area of struggle in your marriage, don't throw some external boundaries, hoping that will fix your problem. It will just aggravate your man. First treat the root of the problem, not the symptoms.

One of the things *you* can do now is to show the way. If you want him to be open with you, be open with him. Let him have access to your phone, if he doesn't. Share your passwords, casually talk about your day mentioning who you talked with. Be what you want to see in your marriage. If trust is a very big challenge, involve a trusted mentor or Christian counselor.

For those who travel a lot, you have to go the extra mile to nurture oneness and openness. Talk to your spouse everyday or as much as you can, preferably via channels where you see or hear one another. Hearing each other's voice nurtures your intimacy in a deeper way, compared to an impersonal text or chat.

Generally when you work on polishing your treasure, when you work on building intimacy and closeness, straying or playing with boundaries becomes much harder. Others will see that you esteem and treasure your marriage and stay clear.

7. Cultivate couple friendships.
It's easier to relate to the opposite gender when you cultivate same couple friendships. It takes out the awkwardness and helps you both relate at a much deeper level as couples.

But some of us wives want to bring all our single-days guy friends into our marriage, even when hubby doesn't like them! Some women say "but we've been friends all our lives, if anything was to have happened, it would have happened a long time ago!"

Well, let's start here; if your guy friend is still trying to be best-buddies with you and not with your husband, that's totally weird. Second, when you said "I do" to your husband, you said "I don't" to all other men. So if your guy friend can't get along with your husband or is not trying to be friends, you need to show him the door. Keep your distance and fade out of his life.

Be about the business of guarding and building up your marriage, not stretching and wearing it down. Seek friendships that build your marriage, not tear it down.

8. If you feel tempted, f.l.e.e.

Remember the story of Joseph in Genesis 39? He ran so fast from Mrs. Potiphar, he left his cloak behind! Joseph wasn't concerned with keeping faces or dignity; when temptation (or better phrased, temptress) came his way, he took off!

If you ever feel tempted to cross your boundaries or if someone tries to seduce you, don't stop to rationalize it, play nice or macho up. Just run! Let's create a scenario.

You are going through a bumpy time at home the same week you have a huge project at work. You get to the office and realize you can't possibly hand the report on time *because* you spent a lot of time trying to work out issues at home the previous night.

"What's up Michele, need some help?" Peter, your colleague. He's always so nice. He scoots over your desk and starts to look through your papers. "So," he continues, "what's really troubling you, you've not been yourself these last few days."

You need some help with the report. Your heart is a mess, and you know you can't trust your mouth, or your eyes not to well up. But Peter is "safe" (married), you tell yourself and continue to debate whether to be honest or modest. "Oh he's being so helpful already, I owe him some honesty."

Obviously you have no impure motives, just office conversations with a colleague.

Or so you tell yourself.

But there's nothing safe or simple about the direction of your conversation. Your best recourse? Don't accept the bait to discuss your private matters. Run.

I know that was no seduction scene, but playing with fire rarely looks or feels like it at the *beginning*. That's why you are careful, why you nip things in the bud so you don't have to rebuild a house burned to the ground, down the road.

You might be very newlywed right now and you are reading this and thinking you are immune. Listen, the devil is no respecter of age in marriage. He hates your vows and will do anything to destroy your marriage. One of the ways he will do that is try to plant seeds of laziness, ignorance and naivety. Don't be ignorant. Draw your boundaries and keep them. Watch your heart now and learn how to stay on "I do" mode.

If this is a big area of struggle in your marriage, please seek accountability fast. Secret sin will fester but "two are better than one, because they have a good reward for their toil. For if they fall, one will lift up his fellow." Ecclesiastes 4:9 ESV

My friend and Author Barb Raveling says "If you're attracted to someone, let a friend know and have that friend hold you accountable to not even thinking about that person."[5]

9. Pray specific prayers
Paul said in 2 Corinthians 10:3-5 "For though we walk in the flesh, we do not war according to the flesh. For the weapons of our warfare are not carnal but mighty in God for pulling down strongholds, casting down arguments and every high thing that exalts itself against the knowledge of God, bringing every thought into captivity to the obedience of Christ."

Connect with God in this area and be specific. Pray over your unity and oneness in marriage. Pray that He would enable you and your husband to keep a guard over your mind and heart. Pray that He would keep your hearts one, glued to Him and fused as one.

10. Think about the consequence of infidelity.
"Big picture thinking" can spur and motivate us to keep proper boundaries in marriage. When you know that life is not all about you, that your actions do indeed have consequences and will affect loved ones

in a big way, you are more careful, more determined to live above reproach.

Keeping Boundaries With Your Family

After marriage, our biological families slide to third place in our lives. We still love and cherish them but as far as that list of priority goes, it's God, then our husbands, then family.

I did not always understand that principle, at least not from experience.

I got engaged on Christmas Eve and danced into my mum's house, nearly jumping out of my skin in excitement. I shared the big news and expected my sisters and mum to jump up and down with me...or at least look happy and say congratulations.

Instead, they looked at me like I'd sprouted leaves from the back of my head. My mum wondered what my shiny ring was all about, whether I'd gotten married and left her out of the wedding! In her days rings were reserved for a wedding ceremony.

I was floored. And angry. It took a long while to piece together what happened that evening.

I would realize that while I was happily skipping out of their lives, they were going through very different emotions as the ones being left.

Here are a few things I later learned from that evening:

1. It's not easy being left
I was announcing an engagement ten months after the death of our dad. My family was not ready to part with another family member. Plus I was the first girl, out of five girls (and I am the last born of nine kids) to walk down the aisle. We just didn't have any experience with the happy and squealing engagement dance.

Maybe your family has different issues. But the bottom line is; it's not easy to let go of a family member. It's important to understand where your family is coming from. That understanding will help you choose cleaving *without* being upset with your family. Your family is not necessarily being mean or trying to make your marriage life complicated, if indeed they are not. They are just trying to figure out their place in your new life. And that process will involve a lot of perplexity, misunderstanding, anxieties, and sometimes downright hardheadedness. So as you understand what is really going on – that they are processing the pain of being left – you will be in a better position to extend empathy even as you leave and cleave with your husband.

2. You leave anyway

While I eventually understood my family's perplexity, I had to make a choice and continue out of the door before that complete understanding. I did not cancel my engagement because my family didn't join my happy-party immediately.

When you accept God's timing and purposes for your life, don't expect everyone to understand and accept right along with you. Don't stop doing what needs to be done. Do it anyway and pray that they catch up with you.

Let's break this down. If they struggled to let you go, don't allow the struggle to continue onto your marriage. I am blessed to have a family that respects and loves my husband and our marriage. Yet I've heard of siblings and parents who refuse to let go of their sister. They wiggled into her marriage and try to call the shots, right down to how her husband should treat her and how she should respond when he doesn't.

You can't stop your family from having an opinion about your marriage or your man. As Martin Luther said, you can't stop a bird from flying over your head, but you can stop it from making a nest in your hair. As a wife, you help your family make a nest in your marriage when you run to them every time you have a bump in your marriage. In that case you can't blame them for nesting, you invited them!

While the two of you will forgive one another and move on, your family won't move on as quickly. So if you don't want their "help," stop asking for it. Instead, look for a real mentor, someone who won't take sides and one who will be rooting for both of you.

Even if your family is loving and supportive of your marriage, quit leaning on them. As long as you are leaning on your family, no matter how awesome they are, it will hinder your unity and growth. In my own marriage I've had moments when I "just want to talk" to my mum or spiritual mum, pick their brains on something. I know both of these women love me and want the best for my marriage. And if anything, since they know me so well, they'd probably side with my husband if I ever went spouting off about him!

But over the years God has been teaching me to seek His wisdom *first*. Think about it, your mum or mentor had to learn what she now knows, right? Chances are she did not learn it from a text book or having someone else do marriage on her behalf. She learned from experience; by going through challenges, seeking God's wisdom, leaning into pain and working through issues with her husband. Without having a third wheel. Yes there those deep chronic issues that need outside intervention from a trusted mentor, pastor or counselor. But even then, it's with the understanding that no one can do marriage and cleaving on your behalf.

3. Be willing to go through the process
I am not the only bride who has ever second guessed her very decision to get married when she encounters storms in the early days. If you are there right now, or have ever been, I want to leave you with this final thought as we wrap up this chapter; it takes growth and trust to deactivate "flight" mode. It takes time to move from "how can I get I out of this, did I make a mistake?" to "How can we work through this, because mistake or not, it must work"

Our "exit" questions are often driven by fear, ignorance, immaturity, even selfishness. We are childish in our thinking because we are young. It's important to understand that position so that when storms come, you don't run yourselves down.

Instead you look forward, knowing that things will change one day. That the more you educate yourself, the less fear will have a grip on you.

And whatever you do, don't make permanent decisions in temporary situations. One day you will grow up. You won't always struggle with the same things. Don't grow weary early.

The cleaving seed that was planted in you after you exchanged your marriage vows must be fanned and nurtured in order to bear much more fruit. Accept the process. Embrace it and cling to God's good promises.

#6

Sex and intimacy in marriage

I am my beloved and my beloved is mine.
Song of Solomon 6:3

As we pointed out earlier, intimacy in marriage goes beyond the physical. It's also a mental, emotional, social and financial connection.

You might be thinking that your husband does not care for these other parts of intimacy, and only thinks about sex.

Here's what one husband has to say:

"A good man wants his wife's heart. He wants relationship. He wants unity – not only of body but unity of spirit. He wants to be one with his wife and he wants her to desire to be one with him. Good men willingly receive from their wives but they are not mere takers. They want their wives to receive from them, too, and receiving involves not merely being present but desiring to be present"[1]

So while it might look like your husband desires physical intimacy more than anything else, mere sex does not satisfy him. He wants all of you, not just some part of you.

We'll go into details shortly but let's first look at these other areas of intimacy.

Spiritual Intimacy

Spiritual intimacy is really *the* foundation for a strong marriage. If you can't agree on spiritual matters, you'll struggle to agree on other things.

Spiritual intimacy involves sharing the same spiritual values, praying and reading God's word together, going to church together, serving together in ministry. It does not mean keeping the same pace as far as spiritual growth is concerned, but it means being in agreement. Typically, wives *can be* more spiritually sensitive than their husbands. As a wife you must appreciate your differences and honor him as the head of your home. Just because you are relational and more attune to spiritual things does not necessarily mean you are more spiritual. I like to think of myself as more sensitive to God's heart while my husband is more sensitive to God's mind!

I tell single ladies to "marry one who dreams their dream." In other words, marry someone who is going your way spiritually and all other areas of life. I tell them to keep in mind that the man will be the head of their home and while that doesn't mean he will be perfect, his decisions and choices will affect them deeply.

Many ladies set themselves up for heartache when they marry outside their spiritual values. Some actually hope that their man will change after marriage but forget that marriage tends to reveal more of who we are, not less. We don't necessarily become better because we get married; we become better because we choose to become better. So the man you marry will still have to make that decision for God. The difference is that you will be tagging along for the ride.

Some of us are familiar with the term "unbelieving believer." This is basically someone who has a form of godliness but is not living out their faith fully. They want the benefits of salvation but not the obedience and sacrifice. Again if you are a single person, you want to give this type of person a wide berth.

If you are married to a non-believer or an unbelieving believer (whether through choice or a result of a backsliding spouse), listen to what Apostle Paul tells the Corinthian church in 1 Corinthians 7:13, 14a, 16a NLT

"And if a believing woman has a husband who is not a believer and he is willing to continue living with her, she must not leave him. For the believing wife brings holiness to her marriage... Don't you wives realize that your husbands might be saved because of you?"

Commit your marriage to God and trust Him to bring change. Don't stop growing and cultivating your relationship with God because your spouse won't. Don't bug him to change; remember how long it took to make a commitment to the Lord, and how the Lord had to work in you. It wasn't an overnight process and you were not pretty. Expect the same of your husband. It will take time. It will take the Lord working in his heart. In the meanwhile, continue to be an example, loving him like Jesus does.

Intellectual Intimacy

This is a mental connection that includes discussing the "big" things of life such as money, bills, kids etc. as well as the "small" things such as what you had to eat, who you met, highlights of your week, the sunset and so on. I've found that the small, seemingly unimportant things can stimulate our minds and connect us in deep ways. Intellectual connection also involves thinking together and dreaming together. It's being intimate in your thoughts and sharing each other's inner world.

Single ladies, a man's mind needs to be one of the most mesmerizing things about him. Don't just go for looks, dig deeper! If you are bored out of your mind *before* marriage, consider the next ten or twenty years together!

Emotional Intimacy

This involves depositing into each other's love banks, speaking each other's love language, nurturing each other's' emotions, being emotionally transparent. It involves bringing down emotional walls and creating a safe place where you can be comfortable being yourself.

Dr Gary Smalley says, "Make it your goal to create a marriage that feels like the safest place on earth."

Social and Recreational Intimacy

This includes doing things together, and cheerfully so! At our house, my husband loves basketball. I am not a big fan of the sport but we often watch games together. I will inundate him with questions and he will cheerfully supply answers. We laugh, cheer and boo teams together. While my husband enjoys a good strong game and can switch sides several times in a game, I like to pick a team at the beginning and stick with it till the end. A lot of times our game-watching is filled with friendly goading as I urge him to pick a side and stick with it. While he makes a point of explaining the importance of two strong teams and the joy of "not being bound by fickle human emotions like picking sides."

You'll find that as you dive into your spouse's world, you won't lack interesting things to talk about!

I am not the only one who seeks to connect with him in his areas of interest. He doesn't like shopping (unless he's going to pick specific items on sale!) but I do. So he tags along and waits patiently, offers practical advice as I cruise the aisles, perusing labels and trying on items.

Social and recreational intimacy will also involve cheering and encouraging each other's individual interests. You don't have to be involved but you can encourage individual pursuits and interests.

I find that as a wife I can be quite reluctant to release my husband to do his own thing. Maybe because I often have my little list of things I want done or I just want to hog all his time and attention! Either way I have learned that releasing him to do his man things, from racing cars on the phone to hanging out with other guys not only builds him as a person but also energizes him for our relationship.

Financial Intimacy

This includes being open about your finances, making financial decisions together and charting your financial future together. At the time of writing this book, my husband is the sole bread winner but before then (before we moved to America) I was running a business. I remember one day being at a crossroads, trying to figure out how to involve my husband in the financial end of things. It was a young business and there wasn't much coming in and I did not want to deluge his time with daily financial happenings. I mentioned my dilemma to one of my girlfriends, who also ran a business, and she told me to continue updating my husband daily.

Later on, I would look back and see that season for what it was; an opportunity to learn financial unity. I am not naturally inclined to make myself accountable. So while keeping daily updates was a chore at the beginning, it taught me to seek financial oneness instead of feeding my separatist tendencies.

I've discovered that sometimes what we call money issues and disagreements are really not money issues at all. All money did was show us up. Its lack or abundance revealed our selfish, self-centered, proud, immature and undisciplined part of ourselves.

God uses all kinds of things to train and refine us. So maybe instead of fighting about money or thinking that money is driving a wedge between the two of you, maybe it's time to study yourselves and begin address the real problem. Start fighting for unity and cut off everything that doesn't edify.

I receive emails from wives who desire deeper financial openness and accountability but their husbands don't. Having differing views on money and how to be open about it can be a real challenge. Since we are dealing with our part as wives, I'd ask you to first pray and ask God to move in your heart. Don't jump on your husband and try to hammer him with all the ways he should become transparent and responsible. Rather surrender your fears and worries and anxieties to God. Then talk to your husband (refer to Communications chapter). Keep talking. Involve trusted mentors if the challenges are severe. Through all of this, you must understand that God is your help and your source, not your husband. Let your actions, words and life preach that.

Physical Intimacy

When it comes to physical intimacy, husbands will generally think about the physical aspect of sex - the touching, seeing and doing part. Wives on the other hand will generally think about the things that come *before* sex - the talking, the admiration and affirmation, the conversation and the closeness.

Where it Begins

I want to track back a little and lay a foundation for where we are going.

I want to talk about sex before marriage.

Many of you reading this book are already married, but you may have unmarried family and friends. Some of you are still single. I want to share my heart in the area of purity or chastity before we move on, in the hope that what I say will encourage you to take a stand as well as equip you as you encourage the unmarried people in your life.

Also as marrieds, sometimes we find ourselves stuck in blues that have their roots all the way back to our single days. And so in order to make sense of where you are, it's important to understand where you have come from.

The online dictionary defines purity as "the condition or quality of being pure; freedom from anything that debases, contaminates, pollutes"

I hope we can all agree from the beginning that sexual purity before marriage is not merely about abstaining from sexual intercourse, even though that's part of it. Sexual purity is about the purity of the whole person - the mind, body and heart.

In our world today, many people have differing opinions on what purity is all about. Some believe that petting, kissing, making out above clothes - really, anything that involves non-penetrative sex - is okay. As long as they don't go "all the way," they are still exercising chastity.

But there's another group that believes that purity is a whole-person thing. They steer clear of any and all activity or thought that might inflame the flesh. You may already have guessed it but I belong in the second group.

Allow me to explain myself.

Contrary to what many people think, the purity dilemma is not a modern day problem. Sometimes we think we've discovered new sin which the ancient world never had to deal with.

But the Bible tells us that there's nothing new under the sun. Our sin and temptations may present differently, but they've been around for a long time.

The church in Corinth had a few questions for Paul in this area and he addressed it in 1 Corinthians 7:8-9 NLT

"So I say to those who aren't married and to widows—it's better to stay unmarried, just as I am. But if they can't control themselves, they should go ahead and marry. It's better to marry than to burn with lust."

Paul says it is better to marry than burn with lust. He did not say it is better to release pent up sexual energy with a boyfriend than to burn with lust. He said, get a husband/wife! Marriage is the only place for sexual expression.

And this is where I miss the whole liberal-purity boat. And happily so, I might add. I don't understand how one can engage in foreplay (that's what petting, kissing, making out is) without being drawn towards someone sexually. That's the whole point of foreplay, isn't it. It's sexual. Humans were not created with an "off" switch in the brain that allows us to do physically stimulating things without the accompanying emotional and sexual response. *Chaste make-out is an oxymoron!*

God is interested with what goes on behind the scenes i.e. our minds, as much as he is interested in what is visible, i.e. our actions.

Here's how it went down in Genesis 6:5

"Then the Lord saw that the wickedness of man was great in the earth, and that every intent of the thoughts of his heart was only evil continually."

Later on in the chapter, we read how God destroyed the earth and all that was in it except Noah and his family and the animals in the ark through the great flood. God destroyed the world not just because of man's evil actions but because of the evil intents of his heart. Thoughts are important to God!

Let's look at another purity challenge.

There's a group of people who feel that the church, and maybe even this writer, have just about exhausted the whole "physical boundaries" sermon. They feel purity teachings should concentrate on matters of the heart and singles should have the freedom to define for themselves acceptable physical boundaries.

You see, I have a problem with that. We are soul, spirit and body. If you are going to talk about the spirit, you better speak about the soul and body too. That's what a wholesome healthy message is - you minister to the whole person, not parts.

Of course there should be as much teaching about the condition of the heart, as there is about the physical. No doubt. After all, outer boundaries originate from inner boundaries. You need to teach the why behind "it's not wise to kiss before marriage."

But we know that just because you teach heart issues doesn't mean the habits will automatically regulate themselves. Someone has to share practical wisdom, alongside inner wisdom.

Boundaries do not save us. We don't keep boundaries and watch our interaction with the opposite sex to earn salvation or be in God's good books. Rather we pursue righteousness and holiness *because* we have been made new by God and because we want to honor Him.

High Standards or Man-Made Rules?

Let me share something my husband wrote in his devotions on this area:

"We must be careful not to mislabel high standards as man-made rules. In John 14:5, Jesus says "if you love Me, you will obey Me". So here's how we should be thinking: "What is God saying to me today? Am I obeying? Am I obeying *promptly*? How can I better *serve, do* and *become* in the will of God? What is best practice in moving from the permissible to the perfect? Am I getting better? Am I content or am I hungry for more? Rules can be static, stagnant, inorganic and punitive. Standards, however, are goals that draw out the dynamic, the growth and a unique freedom within boundaries that the human soul thrives in. These boundaries are drawn by the pursuit of the goal. Boundaries don't form the goal. It is the goal that forms the boundaries. We certainly don't need more rules. We certainly do need a higher standard."

To the unmarried person, yes, God is faithful to keep you from falling into sin. But He will not come down and physically restrain you. He gave you a free will and His grace, not so that you can live however you want to, but so that you would choose Him. He will help you live for Him, He will enable you by the power of the Holy Spirit to wait - and wait well. But you must understand that His grace and mercy is not an out-of-jail card to do what you want. It's really a cue to take up your cross and follow Him.

Why God Wants us to Stay Pure

The world wants us to believe that sex is just a physical thing, an activity between two consenting adults, for recreational purposes and mutual enjoyment. But the Bible paints a different picture.

God created sex for intimacy, for procreation, for companionship and pleasure.[2]

He created sex to bind two individuals in a deep, exclusive union, so deep and unfathomable that it could only be described as one flesh. It's a fusion of not just body but mind and soul. Mark 10:8b says, "So they are no longer two, but one flesh..."

God meant for this kind of unveiling and bonding to happen within a lifelong covenant, one with the highest level of safety, love and trust. He did not design us to become one flesh with several different people, hence all the untold pain, heartbreak and suffering that comes with sex outside marriage. We cannot create one-flesh intimacy with several people.

I don't have experiential perspective on sex outside marriage because I waited, but I can tell you about the joy and peace that comes from waiting. I know we don't like to talk about it because we feel like talking about waiting well automatically condemns anyone who did not wait. But advocating for chastity does not mean you are condemning others. There's a place for balance.

There's a special delight in presenting your body to your mate on your wedding night, without regret or memories from the past. It's so beautiful to accept and enjoy the gift of one another because it's all you've ever known, there are no plan B's and no exes on the scene.

This does not mean that if you did not wait until marriage to have sex, you are locked out of God's plan! No! There is nothing that is too hard for the Lord to heal. Some of you reading this might have had your innocence taken against your will. That breaks the heart of God. Wherever you find yourself, I want you to know that there's healing and redemption for this area of your life. God will heal and restore you if you let Him.

Starting Out

Whether you are a virgin or not, we walk into marriage from different backgrounds, understanding and life experiences.

One person might come into marriage carrying memories of past sexual encounters, unknowingly expecting their spouse to live up to the image in their minds. Another person will come into marriage with zero experience, naively expecting everything to click into place automatically, without any effort or learning. Someone else might be carrying emotional wounds and pain from the past that makes it difficult to experience fulfilling intimacy in marriage.

No matter where you find yourself, I want you to understand that no one comes into marriage perfect. Obviously some pains and challenges are deeper than others. But everyone has a race to run and things to overcome. So don't allow the challenges to overcome you, rather to put on the mindset that you can do everything through Christ that strengthens you.

Adjusting Your Attitudes Towards Sex; For Those Who Waited

For many people who waited to have sex in marriage, sometimes the mental switch can be difficult at the beginning. The main challenge here is that you came into marriage expecting to breeze through because, after all, you waited to have sex and you expect a perfect transition. While some people will have smooth transitions (not perfect), others will not. Like we said earlier, we are all different – different backgrounds, understanding, experiences – and all that plays a part in the bedroom.

Earlier, we saw that the counseling we receive before marriage is a lot like learning how to swim while seated in a classroom. But once married (once you dive into the pool), you get to practice what you learned in class. Sex in marriage is like that too. You may have heard a few things but it was never put into practice.

So for every wife who waited – or every bride in waiting - understand that waiting does not guarantee perfect sex in marriage. You can't just lie there and hope for miracles! You have to learn and apply yourself. Don't quit simply because you hit some unforeseen bedroom blues.

Adjusting Your Attitudes Towards Sex; For Those With Past Sexual Experience

One misconception people have is thinking that past sexual experience makes for better sex in marriage. And maybe that's why some want to push boundaries before marriage - to bag some experience! (Heads up single sisters, if he wants to taste the goods before he buys them, lace up your shoes and run! If he can get it for free, chances are he won't buy the whole package)

Sex before marriage doesn't make you a "pro." If anything, it gives you a lot more issues to overcome once married.

Listen to this one woman's story:

"I had gone so long in unhealthy relationships & having sex outside of marriage that I felt guilty for those first couple months being able to have sex within marriage. I was used to beating myself up after disobeying God that I took that bad way of thinking into my marriage. I had to remind myself that God was with us and that he honored our marriage covenant."[3]

If sex outside marriage has been your story, it's possible to bring that same mentality into marriage. You might be overcome with shame and guilt like the lady above.

Or you might expect fireworks, tumble and play, without the accompanying hard work that goes into building a real committed relationship.

For the bedroom to be successful, other areas of marriage must be working as well. You have to be working on your friendship, cultivating good conflict resolution skills, having fun, enjoying your own individual lives.

If you were sexually active before marriage, don't fall for the lie that you have an upper hand in marriage. Don't sit under a mental palm tree, fantasizing about the "good old days" when everything came easy and you didn't have to work so hard to understand him or when you could "deny" him sex during disagreements.

Let me also point out that not everyone had frills and fun. Some of you are carrying shame and guilt from the past. You are reading this and wondering if there's any hope for you, if things can ever change. God is our healer. While the rest of the world (including yourself) is getting ready to stone you and give up on you, Jesus is extending forgiveness and love right now.

In John 8:1-11, Jesus tells Mary Magdalene, the woman caught in adultery, "Neither do I (condemn you), *go and sin no more.*" (Brackets added)

I encourage you to commit yourself afresh in this new season of your life. Ask God to give you a fresh perspective. Pray that He would reveal the areas and wounds that need to be healed. If you haven't done so, repent of your sexual sin. And then believe that you have been forgiven. Accept God's forgiveness and don't let guilt and condemnation hang over your head and steal the wonderful gift of sex in marriage.

Leap forward and begin to apply yourself. If you need someone to walk you through this, be courageous and find a wise godly woman or mentor to help you and pray with you. Don't assume you are doomed to fail. You are not. Don't allow the past to stop you from experiencing the new thing God has brought into your life. Press forward and find health.

Isaiah 43: 18- 19

"Do not remember the former things, nor consider the things of old. Behold, I will do a new thing, now it shall spring forth; Shall you not know it? I will even make a road in the wilderness And rivers in the desert."

Shedding Passivity & Understanding our Sexual Differences

Great intimacy is a journey. Nonetheless, unless we intentionally engage and apply ourselves from the beginning, the bedroom life doesn't necessarily get better.

I was virgin when I got married. I had done my research, (as much as was appropriate for a single girl anyway) on the topic. After marriage I realized I did not understand my feminine make up one iota.

I wanted my husband to know, instinctively, the right buttons to push to make me happy. I thought as a man, he knew how to make sex feel great and he didn't need input from me. On the other side, my husband was wondering why pleasuring his wife was so laborious! I really had no idea that it takes two to make things work in the bedroom.

Now let me remind you again; it's okay to come into marriage without "experience". That's how it's meant to be! We can't completely understand our sexual nature until we are sexually active and that's fine! If you are single right now, I am not suggesting that you run out and get some experience. God means for us to learn sex within marriage, not outside marriage.

But once married, naivety and ignorance stops being your defense! When we say "I do," we promise to start learning wifehood.

I had other issues too, beside ignorance. Some of the things I have shared in this book are a bit awkward for me to write, but this chapter tops it! But I want to encourage you and let you know that you are not alone, that we all go through the same learning channels and we overcome if we don't give up.

My other challenge was speed. Rather, a lack of speed. While my husband didn't need much to get "in the mood," I needed time - a lot of it - to warm up and get ready for lovemaking.

Being the competitive and naive person I was, I tried to beat my husband to the starting line. I believed that I could warm up faster and I had moments when I pretended I was "there" before I truly was. Again, I hadn't understood how the female body works and I was trying to make my body do something it couldn't. But in the end, I got more frustrated and disappointed. Added to my misery was the fact that I had also convinced myself that my husband was as frustrated with my erratic pace as I was.

It took sometime to understand the root of my frustration; I was ignorant and passive.

We'll look at how to understand your body and how to work through the differences. But first you must understand and *accept* that you and hubby are different and that's okay! Genesis 1:27 says God created them male and female. Genesis 1:31 goes on to say "Then God saw everything that he had made, and indeed it was very good."

You are not a mistake. Just because you can't warm up as quick or don't feel the same way he does or as quickly does not mean you are abnormal. Your difference reveals the majesty and creativity of God.

Without our differences, we would not enter deeper dimensions of relationship. For example, most men *typically* have a higher sex drive than women. As a result, both husband and wife have to work hard to find that fulfilling middle ground. There's a lot of sacrifice for both, stepping out of comfort zones, becoming more tender, more loving, more giving. If there were no differences, there'd be no opportunity to love deeper.

As you notice your differences, make a beeline for your Maker. The bedroom is such an intimate place and it's easy to cross out God all together. But without God, the very Author of sex, you can't make lasting headway.

So start by talking to God. Then start talking and engaging your husband. Don't assume everything will straighten itself out without practical involvement, because it won't. Let your man know what is working and what is not. Let him know when he's too fast, when you need a little more foreplay, spelling out the exact thing you'd like to try or want him to do.

Your one flesh union becomes deeper and sweeter because you both invest yourselves intentionally. There's no place for passivity, no place for the fears it spawns. This marriage candle must burn from both ends!

Sex Begins in the Mind

We miss the entire goal of sexual intimacy in marriage when we start looking at it like a chore, completely disengaged in the mind and just another thing to cross off a long to-do list. Sometimes, we don't know we've engaged chore-mode until we hit sexual blues and start looking at the root of our issues.

As we continue looking at sexual intimacy, please understand that God did not create sex for your husband alone. He created it for you too. You are supposed to enjoy lovemaking! It's not something you do for your husband; it's something you do together and for one another.

Until you realize that it's yours to enjoy, sex will be a chore. A rather pesky one at that, the one that sits right at the bottom of your to do list, right after cleaning your closet (how often do you clean your closet in a year?). If we understood just how much our enjoyment blesses our husbands, we'd purpose to have a mind makeover in this area marriage.

The reason a good head is so important is because unless your mind is in the game, your body will struggle to follow. Typically, wives have it the other way round - we think that our bodies or emotions lead and then our mind follow. In other words, we want to *feel* in the mood before we make love.

But the truth is that for most women sex begins up there in the mind.

Here's how I began to learn that truth:

I walked into our hotel room on our wedding night, tingling from head to toe with the glorious events of the day. The food, the guests, the dancing, the music, the ceremony, the beautiful flowers and decorations - my head was a flame with thoughts from the day. As we got into the "festivities" of the evening, I could not switch off my brain. The hotel room TV was running in the background and it added to the conundrum in my brain. Suffice it to say, I was distracted! I did not know how to switch off the drama and distractions in my head (and room) in order to be in the moment with my husband.

I am not the only wife who has struggled or struggles to switch off distractions of the mind. In fact, my wedding night distresses play across many young marriages today - only with different kinds of clutter and distractions. Unresolved issues from the day, fatigue and stress from work, a long to do list, the call from his mom, the dirty dishes in the sink, and for mamas, a baby in the bed. We drag all these things from our day into our bedroom and we hope to experience great love making.

You can't experience great lovemaking when your mind is on other things. That mental and heart clutter has to be switched off!

When You Don't Feel like Making Love

Sometimes, the problem is much bigger than a mere tuning of minds and hearts to the moment. It is understanding what being "in the mood" is all about. As women, we've believed one too many lies from TV and movies and popular culture, one of them being that women should be all hot and ready at the beginning of lovemaking. You know, like the guys.

The danger here is if you believe you must be swinging from the chandelier right off the gate, you'll think there's something wrong with you when you don't feel like that every time. Consequently, you'll find it easier to excuse yourself out of love-making altogether because..wait for it, you don't *feel* in the mood!

The truth is that most women don't start off at the top of the hill. We begin at the bottom and slowly warm our way up. In other words, when hubby turns to you with a smoldering look after dinner, you are not necessarily feeling like tearing off his clothes in ecstasy. Maybe you feel a little excited and a little sexy especially if you are ovulating, but your body is not ready to go yet. In any case, his desire and yours don't exactly match. But a little while later, with more time and foreplay, your engines will be coming alive.

The problem was not with that initial "I am not feeling in the mood for sex tonight." That's normal because of how you are wired as a woman.

In his book *Sex on the Brain*, Dr. Daniel Amen says,

"Men are always ready for excitement. With lower activity levels in the brain and high testosterone levels, it takes little to get (men) going. They are always idling, waiting to get taken for a ride... Women on the other hand have so much going on in their brains that they need to be soothed, courted and encouraged to be in the mood. They need a *method* to calm down their brains"[4]

Let's look at this "method."

First, God gave us the ability to lead our feelings. We can make our feelings follow intentional actions. Think about that alarm clock and how you smack down the snooze button. You don't always feel like getting out of your warm bed on some days. However, by the end of some of those days, after you got yourself out of bed in the morning, you feel pretty good about some of your achievements. It doesn't matter how you felt in the morning...you still got up, went to the office, did what was expected.

So what's the key to leading your feelings? *Belief.*

The hardest mental step is believing in intimacy when you don't feel intimate. One sure way to awaken and support the belief is to take action, taking actual steps that lead you towards intimacy instead of steps that lead away from intimacy.

Say, for example, that you've had a long day at work or at home, and just about the time you are thinking of crashing into bed, hubby gives you *that* look. Your first thought might be "I can't do this" but since you have been reading this book (hallelujah), you decide to make a mental shift.

You might not be feeling very spiritual at that moment but I suggest you start with prayer. Since God authored sex, it makes sense to talk to him when we experience challenges, right? Nothing loud, long-drawn or fancy, just real talk with God telling him how you feel and asking him to help you with your mind and body and emotions.

As you pray, take practical steps; start leading your feelings. Excuse yourself if you need to, head to the bathroom and freshen up; I don't know how *you* like to freshen up but many wives like their lingerie, nice perfume, scents and candles. As you freshen up, begin to let go of that mental and heart clutter we talked about. Shut the door to your day. Forget about the mile-long to do list and the unfinished project at work.

As you connect with your husband, engage and be present. Tune into your body and enjoy the sensations he stirs in you. The reason you blocked out the clutter is so that you can feel and respond to the present.

This might sound more complicated than it is, and you might think I'm advocating 'faking' through sex and lovemaking. Let me clarify a couple of things:

Intentionally getting yourself in the mood for lovemaking is *not* faking it. We do it all the time in other areas of marriage, doing things for our spouse and our marriage, not because we feel like it, but because we know it's good for our marriage and it yields positive results. We don't consider it faking; we consider it love and maturity.

Secondly, we are all wired differently as women, and not all women will struggle at the beginning *all the time*. But interruptions such as a new job, a baby, a disagreement etc. happen in life and unless we learn how to connect intimately in the midst of those interruptions, we will turn wheels in bluesville forever. We must find a way to do marriage, even in the midst of inconveniences and different circumstances.

My point is; it's possible to get there with just a little more effort. *Do something.* Don't excuse yourself simply because feelings are absent.

Which brings up another point: What if you do all that – the mental shift, intentionally getting ready and engaging in the moment - and sex isn't as wonderful? You know what I am talking about! You freshen up, do your thing, but your mind and body refuse to cooperate, what's a girl to do?

Well, here's what you'll do. *Rest in the assurance that you did not settle for average.*

Fireworks are good, but they are not everything. For us wives, there's a sweetness and closeness, an aroma, a depth and refreshing that's nurtured each time we connect intimately with our husbands.

While quality lovemaking is important, understand that you won't always enjoy a sumptuous six-course meal! Sometimes we'll order take-out and that's okay!

When Sex is Not Possible

There may be days when you are tired or unwell or some other reason and making love is not an option. That's perfectly okay. However, there should be more "yes" than "nos" in your sex life and the "no" should always be lovingly communicated (because clearly your husband missed the cue that you might be too tired or unwell.)

Even when sex is not possible, think about other ways to still connect without it. This could include cuddling, snuggling, kissing.

If you are struggling with past sexual abuse or lovemaking is painful - in other words the issues are much deeper than "not in the mood," I encourage you to find professional help, talk to your pastor or trusted mentor and begin to get healthy in this area.

Preparing for Lovemaking

As a wife and when you have guests coming over for dinner, you almost always take time to think about what you will cook. You don't throw things together and hope for a miracle! You go out to the stores and shop for some good ingredients. Then you take the time to prepare the ingredients: wash, skin, cut, marinate, blanch, the works. Then you follow a certain recipe. You make sure the dish is not over salted, you stir as needed, you watch over that pot; basically, you stay engaged until the food is ready and served to your guests. Then you sit back and enjoy the compliments and satisfied happy looks from your visitors.

Think about lovemaking the same way. You can't be harried and haphazard and expect a delightful "amen!" from either of you! You have to take time and prepare.

Here are a few thoughts on preparation:

1. Your bedroom.
It should be a refuge, a peaceful inviting oasis for you and your husband. Keep it clean and fresh. Change the beddings often. You don't need expensive beddings, fancy wall decorations or furniture to make a sweet restful retreat. Just work with what you have.

For a start, put those clothes back into the closet! Remove the workstation from the bedroom and take it to the kitchen or living room. Let your bedroom be all about you and your husband, not about work. (On the side; my husband and I recently moved to a smaller house and we've had to transform one corner of our bedroom into a small office. But even so, we've created a very deliberate marker between the work area and the rest of the bedroom. So if you have to work from your bedroom, you can still create a clear distinction between the work area and the rest of your bedroom)

At our house, we also decided we'll never have a TV in our bedroom. Because TV feels a lot like a third person (a strange intrusion!) in the most private intimate room in the house. When we want to watch a movie in bed, we bring in the laptop or tablet; these are not permanent fixtures.

Think about ways to make your bedroom a private, inviting and restful oasis for just the two of you.

2. Your mindset.
You don't start making the meal when your guests are seated on your dining table waiting for dinner. In the same way, you can't wait till

the last minute to start thinking about sex. Begin thinking about sex much earlier, during the day! Spare a minute or two (or ten!) to think about yourselves. Linger on there, what you like, how he makes you feel, what he did last night. Think about what you need to do today to have *that* again. Maybe you need to get home earlier to fix dinner so you can have more relaxed time together.

Make a habit of thinking about sex, not just *right before* you make love, but long before then. Learn to put yourself in a proper frame of mind, build anticipation.

Listen to this woman building anticipation for her man:

Song of Solomon 3:1 – 4

"By night on my bed I sought the one I love; I sought him, but I did not find him. "I will rise now," I said, "And go about the city; in the streets and in the squares I will seek the one I love." I sought him, but I did not find him. The watchmen who go about the city found me; I said, "Have you seen the one I love?" Scarcely had I passed by them, when I found the one I love. I held him and would not let him go..."

3. Your initiative

When we were about two years married and going through some blue-colored patches, I asked one of my mentors whose responsibility it was to text more during the day. To be honest, I just wanted to hear that it was my husband's responsibility, that it was his job to pursue me and put all the effort to keep romance alive.

Her answer shocked me. "Text him. You both must be texting one another".

It took a while for that to sink in. That while my husband was the leader of our home, I was his partner. We *both* had to put in the effort to make romance flourish!

It's the same advice I have for you; don't leave it to your husband to do all the work in the bedroom! Flirt with him. Send him messages (while keeping the more sexy details in code of course!) Let him know you find him attractive, that you want him. When he does something right, tell him - with sound and expression. Be *nice* in your communication - don't grunt and push him away when he does something unexciting, be sweet in your communication.

Interesting thing is, the more you celebrate something, the more you fall in love with it! What you magnify becomes bigger and better in your eyes!

4. Your creative efforts
If you've had a long tiring day at work, try and catch fifteen minutes of alone time to re-energize. Don't use tiredness as an excuse if there's something you can do about it. Get into that bathroom, freshen up, begin to get your mind into intimacy mode. A shower or bath after a long day can completely change your frame of mind as your body relaxes. Put on some nice perfume or lotion. Wear nice lingerie instead of your usual functional fare.

The bottom line? Work yourself into the mood instead of waiting for your husband to do the work for you. There's nothing your husband can do to get you in the mood, unless you cooperate.

When He Doesn't Want Sex

Let's change gears a bit. A lot of intimacy advice is geared towards helping wives want more sex. And there's nothing wrong with that approach because women typically need that kind of encouragement. We are "delicate" and one small thing can throw us out of balance and affect our sex drive. So we need a lot of information, encouragement and equipping.

But there's another group of women who need a different kind of encouragement. Current statistics put the number of marriages with a higher libido wife and a lower libido husband at about 30%.

There are various reasons a husband would have low libido. These include illness, low testosterone, unresolved inner issues like anger or self-worth, past sexual abuse, stress, addictions, pornography or depression. It could also be the result of a wife who previously rejected her husband and her man learned to shut down.

If you are a higher libido wife with a low libido husband, I'd like you to write this somewhere in your heart;

"How I phrase my concern about an unsatisfying sex life will determine if my husband will open up and talk to me or shut down and withdraw."

If you think that statement is skewed in his favor, think about other areas of marriage where you need his understanding. For example, how he phrases an ongoing concern will determine if you feel loved or rejected, which in turn influences your willingness to cooperate and find a solution together.

Now typically, (I use the word *typically* because not all husbands feel exactly this way, though many husbands do) and no matter what you think, your man's sense of manhood and completeness is closely tied to his performance in the bedroom; he feels good about himself when he's able to satisfy his wife sexually.

The opposite is true: he feels terrible when he's unable to perform. And his suffering is greater than you can fathom.

If you are in this position right now, I want you to consider the following:

1. You are not abnormal for wanting sex
The prevailing thinking is that wives want less sex, and so there's a wealth of advice on how to want it more. You might have tried to put all that advice into practice but nothing catches your husband attention. In fact, some of the things you do, the ones touted to make you more desirable, turn him off.

As is typical with most women, when things aren't working out to everyone's satisfaction, especially in intimate matters, our first thought is to believe *we* are the problem. So here you are working harder, dressing sexier, pursuing harder thinking that you can make it change.

You've build up expectation and hope, but since you are not the primary problem, nothing changes and you crash. You irritate the one with the problem because now they feel like a project. In the end you are caught up in a roller coaster that not only affects your marriage but it also devastates your esteem and confidence as a woman.

Hear me wife; you are not abnormal for wanting healthy sex in your marriage. God made sex; you did not think it up! God wants you to thrive in your marriage, the bedroom included, and you are not abnormal for wanting health there.

As long as you keep blaming yourself and thinking up all the ways you can fix it and make it better, you will not make progress. Quit approaching your challenges as if you are the problem. Certainly, you have a responsibility to work together. But you do so with understanding and peace, not with guilt and shame and a false sense of responsibility.

2. Sort yourself before you try to sort him out
Your husband's sexual challenges, especially if prolonged, may have left you feeling rejected and unwanted. More so if he's been unwilling (most probably unable) to talk about it. You are probably angry and frustrated and want to lash out and to blame.

Instead of acting out your anger, frustrations and fears, ask God to help you live out 1 Corinthians 13:4-8
"Love suffers long and is kind; love does not envy; love does not parade itself, is not puffed up; does not behave rudely, does not seek its own, is not provoked, thinks no evil; does not rejoice in iniquity, but rejoices in the truth; bears all things, believes all things, hopes all things, endures all things. Love never fails."

You might not like what I am about to say but it's true. One of the reasons you are angry and frustrated is because deep down, you have been expecting your husband to be God. You look to him to build your worth, make you feel loved and accepted, soothe your fears, give your "rights" as a wife and make you feel whole.

It is true that God has given you this earthly relationship to meet some of the needs He hardwired in you. But this gift (your husband) is not meant to replace Him. We were never meant to take our eyes and affection off God. Whether your husband is making love to you or not, you are complete in God. Process your emotions from that angle; that God loves you and in Him, you have everything you need. Go to Him for filling, not to your husband.

As God fills you to overflowing, you are able to go the extra mile in your marriage, to love your husband as God does. And because He met all your needs, you release your husband from that high responsibility of making you whole.

3. Pursue a higher road

Perhaps you feel that no understands you. The church circles certainly don't talk about the sexually unfulfilled wife. Maybe you tried to share with a close friend, only to be met with a light "I envy you! I wish mine didn't want it so much!" It was a joke, you laughed. But it hurt because it made you feel like the odd one out yet again, and also cemented what you secretly think – that there's no hope.

You must shake yourself out of this hole of blues. Rise above the mindsets and perceptions that are trying to kill your hope.

No one is exempt from sexual challenges, even couples in the early years of marriage. You just don't know it because many people aren't talking about it.

So don't wait for someone else to fix your marriage for you. Yes, that's what you are doing right now, sitting there and waiting for someone to cheer you towards solutions and getting all hopeless and depressed when they don't.

Shake yourself and get proactive. Begin to read articles and books on how to deal with sexual challenges in the bedroom.[5]

More than anything else, get into the word of God and learn what He says about you, your marriage and your husband. Spend time in prayer and worship. Immerse yourself in God and allow Him to transform and empower you. Whatever you do, don't sit there and hold a pity party. God and you are a majority. You might be young in marriage but your God is not. He's been around for a mighty long time and He knows how to make things work.

4. Learn to draw him out.

Much as you believe you understand what's going on with your husband, you really have no clue. You don't understand the depth of his frustration and fear and anxiety. I am talking about husbands who actually feel bad about the situation, not someone who has intentionally turned away to e.g porn, and is no longer interested in pleasing his wife. A man who wants to please his wife will feel bad when he can't. And to have this happen in the early years of marriage is crushing.

That's why as his wife you must pray because you can't do it alone. You can't hold your husband to make him feel better. You can't be sexy enough to make him want you. As we said earlier, sometimes the more you try, the more frustrating it is for both of you. Don't assume you know what he's going through. Don't take things lightly because in his world, things are heavy.

Proverbs 31:26 NASB has this to say about the wife of noble character. "She opens her mouth with wisdom, and the teaching of kindness is on her tongue."

Wisdom will open doors that pain and devastation have shut. Wisdom is gentle and quiet. It does not demand its way, it's not self-seeking. Marriage has its gifts and blessings, but a wise woman will easily relinquish those, even temporarily, for the good of her marriage.

James 1:5 NIV says "If any of you lacks wisdom, you should ask God, who gives generously to all without finding fault, and it will be given to you."

You might feel ill-equipped to handle the task before you but ask God to supply what you lack.

I am harping on wisdom here because without it, you won't be able to seek out your husband's heart. You won't approach the issue with the sensitivity and love it needs.

When addressing the issue with your husband, temper your words. Be patient and seek to understand, as opposed to trying to drill a point home. Don't go on a diatribe on the whole problem - no one wants to discuss their weakness and challenges the whole night. Be sensitive and know when he's had enough. Pick up that conversation a later time. As you talk, approach it from the angle of love - reassure him and coat your words with love.

5. Cultivate friendship

There's no challenge a couple cannot overcome if they cultivate their friendship. Obviously cultivating a friendship is more difficult when you are going through difficult times. As humans, we focus on the most painful itch, the area of brokenness, not where there's a semblance of peace. It's easy to ignore the rest of marriage as you let yourself be bogged down by issues.

If you can't think one positive thing about your marriage right now, I'd like for you to put this book down and go find one. And if you can't find it, *create one*. Do something for him today, sow a seed of love!
Cultivating friendship means that you decided that you and your husband are a team; whatever comes against one of you meets both of you.

Friends look out for each other; they are not in the relationship for what they can get out of it. You want to hang up your "rights" coat; let the boat of "you owe me" sail down the river. Rise above your issues. Laugh with him, play together, go out on dates, make his favorite meal, do the things he likes. Make your life more than just the bedroom.

As you do, you will begin to realize that it's easier to discuss things with a friend. Because friends don't keep scores. Friends don't put up fences and heavy doors. When you are not feeling judged, but instead are feeling accepted, it's easier to open up. The opposite is also true- when there's a dark ominous cloud in the form of an angry, resentful wife, you want to close up and hide.

6. It will take time
Anything worth having in marriage is worth fighting for. It will take time to fix this area of your life. Even if it's something that can be fixed medically, it might still take time to heal the mind and heart. Especially yours.

Don't allow pride and fear to keep you from seeking outside help. Talk to your mentors, seek professional or medical help. But with it also understand that you still have to go back home and work it through with your man.

As you walk through all this, remember that God honors His word. He said that if we ask we shall receive. It might take time, but it doesn't mean it will never come to pass.

Keep your hopes and dreams at the feet of Jesus. (Psalm 55:22) and leave them there. Don't pick up what you gave to Him. Keep practicing what you are learning and the things He's opening up to you.

Special Notes for the New Bride and Bride-to-be (and Refresher Tips for the Older Bride!)

I can't wrap up the chapter without sharing specific tips with the *very* brand new bride and the bride to be. For the slightly older bride, allow the words to bring sweet refreshing to your own marriage!

• It might be uncomfortable the first time
For most virgins, making love for the first time is uncomfortable. If you

aren't married yet, that's not meant to scare you, it's just a fact.

Christian marriage and sex Author J Parker has this to say concerning sex on the first night:

"You will be sore, just like you were after your first aerobics class. Hey, you're using muscles you haven't used before. What do you expect? But just like exercise, you shouldn't respond by deciding it hurts too much that you have to stop doing it. Be gentle, be careful, but keep up the "exercise." Your body will get used to it, and sex will no longer hurt."[6]

Typically, the discomfort could last until your body and muscles get used to love making and moving in ways it wasn't used to before. If you have severe discomfort and pain, please talk to your doctor immediately, and with a close mentor.

• Lube it!
Don't be afraid to use lubrication aids like KY Jelly, which are available in most stores and pharmacies. Using lubrication doesn't make you less of a woman or your husband less of a man. It's just an aid to make penetration easier. Your body will begin to produce its own lubrication but it might need a little help at the beginning.

I would advise you to read your labels and know what works for your body. For example, you want to avoid lubrication aids that have glycerin as one of the ingredients because it can cause infections.
Artificial lubrication is not just for new brides. Don't ditch it because you are two months married! You'll discover that hormonal changes and fluctuations (especially if you are on some type of hormonal birth control) can leave you a little dry and needing extra lubrication.

• Be patient
You are new at lovemaking; don't be too hard on yourself. Put on a student's cap and decide that you are going to enjoy the learning process! Marriage itself is one long school, from which you never really graduate. So get comfortable in your student's seat! Don't stop having sex because it's uncomfortable! Unless of course there's a problem and you

need to see a doctor.

Otherwise take a break (please take a break) when you need to, but get back to it. Practice makes you better. Communicate with your husband and be gentle with one another. A groom who is encouraging, reassuring, patient and gentle will help his bride overcome her fears and awkwardness, which is key to helping her body relax so that pain-free penetration and lovemaking can be achieved. So communicate with your groom and let him know what you need and how you feel.

• **Understand your groom**
You might not know this about your husband, but unconsciously he believes he has what it takes to pleasure and fulfill his woman.

He might also have come into marriage expecting hot steamy sex for his wedding night… and every night after that. Instead, he finds a clumsy, uncomfortable, awkward experience. Why? Because he did not anticipate his own butterflies or a shy bride or fatigue. He hadn't factored in the magnitude of the mental, emotional and physical difference that exist between himself and his new bride.

Why is this important to you as a wife? Because you need to understand where he is coming from. Before you chart a way forward as a couple, you need to have a good grasp of where you are.

Your man has dreams (as you do too) and your job is not smash them and drag him back to reality. It's to work together as a team, with understanding and love, knowing where the other person is coming from and charting a way forward.

• **He might be more exploratory.**
Husbands like to try out different things, different styles. They are visual and enjoy different kinds of stimulation and variety. But we wives are different. Once we find something that works, like maybe a good position, we like to camp there. Because we need repetitive stimulation, we don't like to change things up every few minutes. And so it's important for your husband to understand that. And you are the only one that

can help..so communicate what you need! Learn and grow together.

• Close the doors to the past
Sex really involves receiving your husband, not just into your body but your soul.

If you had consensual sex before marriage, you opened yourself up and allowed someone into your most intimate part. Their departure - because sex outside marriage always has a departure - left its mark on you. And sometimes when you start being intimate with your husband, that brokenness and wound will start to break open again. Unless you deal with the past permanently you'll continue to struggle to fully trust and cleave to your husband.

As you approach your wedding night and as you grow in marriage, don't ignore the past. Don't stuff things down, hoping they will go away by themselves. Deal with them so you can enjoy real intimacy.

• Then there was makeup sex
Wherever you have conflict, and even when you haven't completely ironed out your differences, seek to come together. I can't explain it but love making will weave your hearts in deep profound ways. When you have issues and fluff in the air, coming together can lower your defenses and level out that "right to be right" monster. Connecting helps you start to see things you weren't able to see before i.e each other's point of view.

So once in a while (or not- so-once-in-a-while), instead of staying up half the night trying to work out challenges, driving each other crazy, head on to the bedroom. Don't shut him down when he reaches for you in the middle of the night after an unresolved conflict. Don't wait to be in the mood. Twist things around and see how that works for your relationship.

• It's awkward at the beginning but you get better with time (as you apply yourselves).
I had no idea that one can kiss and breath at the same time! So on my

wedding night I held my breath… and nearly fainted! Okay I did not nearly faint, but my breathless thereafter was not merely a result of er, you know.

As you approach your wedding, don't expect love making to be a clean, surgical-precise experience. Because it's not. In fact, it can be hilarious! Your delicate lingerie might snap, you might fall off the bed, you might dislike the feel of lubricant, you might gawk, feel embarrassed till your toes curl. (Hopefully not all of them in the same night!)

It's all part of the journey. These awkward moments provide opportunities to be open and vulnerable with one another. Take things lightly. Laugh *together* (not at each other!). Be ready to learn but don't take yourselves too seriously.

• **Keep talking.**
We've already talked about passivity and how to shed it off but it's worth repeating here. There's no other place where wives hope their husbands will read their minds more, than the marriage bed. But the marriage bed happens to be one of those areas where a guy can get it all wrong unless the wife communicates. Remember that he's different from you and unless you tell him what you need, he will keep giving you what he *thinks* you need! And that's not always a good thing.

Don't deliver a whole thesis in the middle of lovemaking of course. But figure out ways to let him know what's going on with you. If it hurts or you want to try something else or if you are sore and want a break for a few hours, tell him.

Don't fall for the lie that "he's the man, he'll figure it out" He won't figure it out because he doesn't live in your brain. And even if he did, his brain works very differently!

Be kind in your communication, offering loving suggestions, not harsh critical rebukes.

• The wedding night is not the end, but the start of your life together
You don't have to have a perfect wedding night. In fact, most couples will tell you, they did not have a picture-perfect wedding night. But they loved it!

With all its little embarrassments and issues, it was the start of their married life and they wouldn't trade the experience for anything. There's so much to be grateful for and so much to look forward to. So don't exchange the joy and fun for perfect! Your wedding night is not all you have, there are hundreds of nights to come.

• Keep a mentor
God designed us to do life with real people. This book and every other resource out there is meant to complement real life relationships, not replace them. You need a trustworthy woman mentor to provide a sounding board, accountability, encouragement in marriage.

I am not suggesting that you need to share all the intimates of your bedroom. No. But all girls have girl-stuff. Questions, clarifications - things that furrow your brow. You need a grounded person, someone who's been there/is there. Someone who knows you in real life. Don't take off after the wedding. Cultivate that relationship and take advantage of it.

As someone who has mentored singles and marrieds for years, I can tell you that good mentors love to help. So it's not like you are imposing on them when you seek answers and clarifications or just want to get together for coffee. Don't keep quiet with struggles, if any. Open up.

It is worth emphasizing that you should choose your mentor well. They must be God-fearing, balanced – she calls you out real quick! -, loves marriage and has a thriving marriage herself.
And always remember to talk to God *first* and people second!

Wrapping Up

Intimacy in marriage is a journey, not an event. You never really arrive, because both of you are constantly growing and changing and so is the relationship. Someone said that it's easier to change the course of a moving car, than to try and change the direction of a stationary one.

In the same way, God can work with an honest couple, one that is willing to admit where they are and are ready to look to Him to get where they need to be. There is no shame in growth!

7

Dealing with financial strains

"The real measure of your wealth is how much you'd be worth if you lost all your money."

Unknown

Experts say that one of the biggest areas of conflict in the early years of marriage is finances. By the time we get married, we've learned to see things a certain way, and that includes how we handle our finances. Sadly, in many cases, we believe our way is better, or the only way.

Unfortunately or fortunately, we marry our opposites. Sue the saver will be attracted to Steve the Spender's carefree, giving spirit. Steve will be enthralled by Sue's faithfulness and ability to stretch the dollar.

But soon after marriage, Steve's carefree attitude will begin to irritate and scare Sue.

"Why don't you put a little money into savings?" She'll want to know.

"But we don't have much left after paying bills and everything else," Steve will answer, "Plus you are only newlyweds once... let's enjoy ourselves!"

Sue will quickly point out areas they could cut back to free up some money for savings. As always, she's specific:

"Why don't you find a less expensive place to hang out with the guys? That might save you some money when it's your turn to buy lunch next time. We could also forego this year's anniversary getaway..."

Instead of being encouraged by her astuteness, Steve is floored. His wife comes across as a nitpicking, no-fun, hoarder.

I am guessing you can see a little bit of Sue or Steve in your marriage. Maybe not to extremes, but you both look at money differently. You have very different ideas on how to spend money, when to save it and how to give it away.

I have found these three things helpful when it comes to finding a common ground and making sense out of your cents:

1. Talk about it

Ideally, the best time to have productive discussions about money is when lack is *not* snapping at your heels.

If you start a heavy discussion when tensions are high, chances are you won't have the emotional and mental margin. Not that you can't bring up money issues when things are charged, if there's urgent need. But it's more important to start money conversations *before* then.

The easier discussions provide an opportunity to communicate your heart, to listen to his and map a way forward. You'll need to keep an open mind and be willing to see things differently, adjust your views and accommodate one another.

Keep in mind that marriage is for the long haul and one conversation cannot do. Seasons come and go and so do our thoughts and perspectives. What was comfortable three years ago might not be okay today and we need to understand and adapt accordingly.

The one thing that will determine how you order your money - and all your life really - is your unique vision (your priorities, values, life direction) as a couple. When you develop your vision as a couple, you establish a common motivation. It then becomes easier to cheer each other towards the common goal and to keep each other accountable.

For example, Steve the spender will remind Sue the saver that they need a fun-filled marriage. Taking a vacation once a year is living out that vision. Sue can remind Steve about their financial vision and can encourage habits and plans that build towards the vision.

2. Understand that he cares

Earlier we looked at the husband's role in marriage and established that he's been charged with taking care of his family, whether his wife has a paycheck or not.

I know there are situations when a husband is home for a season, maybe due to temporary work situations, being laid off or an illness. But overall, being out of work - employment or business - is meant to be a temporary situation, not a permanent lifestyle. A man needs to take care of his family (1 Timothy 5:8) and most husbands want to provide.

I find that as wives and because we are wired to want security, it's easy to believe that we care about our family's financial security more than our husband. Now maybe some of you are married to Spending Steve and you need to have a sober discussion about money. Still, even as you do, you need to remember that Steve wants to make you happy and provide for you. He might not be all savvy about saving and being thrifty, but he wants to provide and meet his obligations.

Don't allow yourself to get upset over your husband's "easy" attitude towards the family's financial future. Just because he's not fussing and talking about the future as much as you are does not mean he doesn't care. Absolutely have the necessarily conversations, but at some point, you have to trust the man. You can't keep bugging and nagging him, hoping to inspire change. When you find yourself starting to worry and nag, you need to wind down and get with God. God is the one that holds your future, not your man.

3. Be practical
You can talk all the way to the moon and back but unless you put some things into practice, it doesn't count towards unity in this area. The goal here is to be one, to be united behind your financial goals and dreams. Once you prayerfully decide what those are, you must carefully adhere to them.

If you draw up a budget stick to it. Don't shop outside your budget using a credit card, and if you do, don't hide the statements from your husband! Be open about it and work from there.

The bottom line is that you have to put to practice the things you agree on. Don't talk one way and act another way. Be consistent.

Going Through Job Loss/Business Struggles

One of the hardest things to go through as a young couple is financial struggles occasioned by job loss or business challenges.

Financial difficulties are hard, no matter how long a couple has been married. But they are especially hard on younger couples because these couples haven't developed enough relational muscle to weather harsh storms.

My husband lost his job four months after our wedding. I was also unemployed, having left my employer of many years three months to our wedding.

I was quickly inundated with insane feelings and thoughts.

• **The situation felt permanent, like things will never change.**
Yes, I had faith for better days, but some days the faith wasn't there.

• **I felt frustrated**
As our struggles wore on, I remember thinking "he's the man, he should have figured it out by now!" My need for cover and security beat up all reason and sense.

• **I was mad with God**
Why us? Why now? What have we done wrong?

• **I was envious of others who weren't struggling**
I had big plans and ideas as most earlyweds do and all of them required some sort of financially stability. When others seemed to do effortlessly what I couldn't do intentionally, envy tried to take root.

Over time I would discover that I didn't have to be held captive by my fears and human reasoning. I could overcome those feelings of devastation and hopelessness by staying rooted in God and speaking His word, not my fears.

If you are going through financial challenges or difficulties in your marriage, here's a few ways to deal with them;

1. Pray for your husband
While he's been charged with the responsibility to provide, he's really only a delegated authority; he's a steward, not the Source.

One of the blessed gifts of troubled financial times is the gift of recalibration of heart. God can begin to form your heart, move you from expecting your husband to have miraculous answers and solutions, to looking to God alone for your answers.

Psalm 54:4 NIV "Surely God is my help; the Lord is the one who sustains me."

During this season, learn to take your (plural) needs to the Lord *first.*

And don't just pray for the visible needs; pray that God would lift up the burden and fill your husband with wisdom and courage and strength.

You'll find that as you talk and immerse yourself in God, fear and anxiety will begin to lose their hold on you. You will have the grace and confidence to walk through harsh financial times with peace and joy.

2. Give extra grace
Chances are your husband is not his usual self during this season.
With the benefit of hindsight, I can see how some of the difficulties we went through in early marriage were a result of a difficult financial season. Back then I did not understand that when men are stressed they migrate to a different stratosphere - they are not as jovial, patient or loving. (and come to think of it, neither are we.) Many lose interest in activities that were previously exciting. As an early wed wife you might see all these personality changes and begin to think they are permanent. Or that he was pretending to be someone else before marriage and now his real colors are coming out.

I am not suggesting that your husband has a free pass during troubling financial times, that he can treat you any way he wants and its okay. Not at all. A good marriage is work, 24/7/365 and both of you must be working on being your best selves no matter what is going on.

All I am suggesting is that *you* can minister love and make both your lives easier by not taking everything personally. Simple things, like not getting irritated by every little thing he does or does not do. Big things like adjusting your mindset and lifestyle to a leaner budget and a simpler lifestyle.

When your husband doesn't have a smile of his own, don't breeze by him and mull over how dull your relationship has become. Give him your own smile, top it off with a kiss, sing praise songs around the house. Become a peaceful oasis in his life, an encourager and blessing who does not pull him down but pulls him up.

Proverbs 17:22 says "A merry heart does good, like medicine, But a broken spirit dries the bones."

The grace you give your husband today will come back to you in your time of need!

3. Think outside the box
By the time my husband lost his job, I was volunteering full time at a Christian organization.

When he was let go, we had to stop, re-strategize and chart afresh. There were bills to pay, huge dreams to weep over and a four-month old marriage to mind. Eventually my husband would get into business and I also started a small business from home.

Going the business route was tough because we both came from corporate backgrounds. Hustling to get the money in and pay the bills was rough. But we were desperate to make ends meet and were willing to try out new things.

It's said that necessity is often the mother of invention. Lean financial times can be the trigger and starting point to greater things in life. Sometimes we don't achieve much because we haven't lacked much. Our lives are filled to the brim, propped up with all kinds of comforts and accomplishments. I have learned that very often God will strip us of *something* in preparation for the next thing. In fact, it's that stripping that makes us yearn for the next level, as our former cushy place stops being so comfortable and we want out!

God doesn't strip us because He enjoys our suffering or discomfort. He strips us because that's the only way to deposit the necessarily wisdom needed for the next level. Greater positions and responsibilities require malleable hearts and difficult seasons have a way of making us soft and pliable. We are more alert to His voice, more willing to do things that we normally wouldn't normally do.

Bishop TD Jakes says that many people who accomplish great things would not have done so but for the fires of hell licking their heels. Great troubles catapult people to great victories.

In your season of difficulty, stay close to God and be ready to step out of the box. He might lead you to new uncomfortable frontiers. Don't sit there in the desert and mourn for Egypt. Don't abort the dreams and hopes He gave you in more pleasant times.

Some of us are silent entrepreneurs who need just a little push. Your husband's job loss - or your own job loss - might be the very thing you need to get your engines going! As you think outside the box, you want to think practical. What is the closest opportunity you can touch, and what can you do right now?

Do you have some free time in your hands? Maybe you could babysit for someone. Are you good with your hands? Then you could create things. Are you good with computers? Spread the word and let people know.

The goal here is to think outside the box in order to bring in that extra income.

If you go on and start something, don't look down on your small efforts and beginnings. You will not always be there.

My home business was actually a hand-made jewelry venture. I started by making little creative pieces and sold them to my friends. It was tough, but I had tougher needs and so I pretty much closed my ears to what people said. After many months, business picked up, enough to help me partner with some friends and open a small outlet in the city. Eventually I added clothing to my line of products. After a year or so, my husband and I partnered with some other friends and opened an office and I started consulting and training. I am telling you this to show you that the first step is often the scariest. If I had been too afraid (or not desperate enough) to start that jewelry business, I would not have opened the consultancy. And I would not be where I am today.

Every small step adds up and leads to something bigger. You don't accomplish big dreams through making one giant leap but through small, intentional, sometimes insignificant-looking steps.

4. Curb your spending (and watch your mouth too)
Lean times can teach you the difference between needs and wants, if you'll listen.

I wasn't attentive at first. My dreams of decorating my new house and updating my wardrobe were up there together with rent and food. I had to quickly learn that new clothes were not in the same category as rent! I had to learn how to steward what we had and adjust my spending habits accordingly, even as I trusted God for more. I could not buy random things and toss in a spiritual "God-will-provide"; that was just an excuse for irresponsible spending.

I also learned that there were other things to rein in, not just spending habits. Women tend to dream with their mouths wide open! We have big plans and lots of ideas and sometimes we don't realize how our endless verbalized longings affect our husbands, who are already feeling the unending pressure to provide.

It's fine to dream! Please keep dreaming, keep expecting and trusting God for the next level.

But be sensitive. Understand where you husband is at. You don't have to ooh and aah over every display on every shopping window.

5. Continue to give

Heaven's math is very different from earth's math. Here, we like to hold on to what we have because we think *one plus one equals two*. But God tends to think *one minus one equals more*. In other words, when you give what's in your hands, you get more. That's how He made us, to be channels, not reservoirs. As long as our hearts stay open, even in drought, He'll give us something to share with others. (Luke 21:1-4)

When God asks us to share during our hardships, He's not asking us to do something He has not done Himself. Jesus was His only begotten son, all He had. But He gave Him up freely for our redemption. He knows what it means to give till it hurts, to give the dearest and closest, *to give everything*. We can't even begin to fathom that kind of giving. But we can surely trust the One who did it and in turn asks us to do the same.

God is no man's debtor, and He doesn't owe us humans anything. When you obey His word, it will bear fruit. (Isaiah 55:11) You might not see the fruit today but once the seed is in the soil and you keep watering the ground like you are supposed to, with faith and actions, your seed will produce a harvest.

To be clear, I am not talking about an imbalanced "prosperity gospel." I am not saying "sow a mango seed" (money) and you will reap 1-2-3 mangoes tomorrow. I believe as Christians, we cannot dictate the kind of harvest we get for our "labor" or obedience. Sure we make our requests known to God. (Philippians 4:6-7) But God is not obligated to answer in ways we understand all the time. His ways and thoughts are higher than ours and that will be clear in our financial walk as well.

Beyond that I've found that God's answers and rewards overshoot my fervent initial prayers and thoughts. He is a good Daddy who loves to give good gifts to his kids, just not always in the ways the kids expect.

Also, giving is not always about money.

As a newlywed, I did not have any money to give. But I had clothes. In fact God took the lesson further by instructing me to give away my favorite clothes. I didn't have a lavish wardrobe to begin with and I knew I was not getting anything new immediately. I remember standing in front of my closet, debating which clothes to give and I heard God say, how about you give all the best ones? I had the opportunity to learn how to give the best without expecting to receive anything in return immediately.

So think about your time, your gifts and talents, what you have in your house. There's always something to give if you look hard enough. But you must be intentional about it and have continued discussions with your husband.

If we allow it, God can teach us to become better givers during lean financial times; lessons learned in painful seasons can last longer than those learned in abundance.

6. Keep a "this too shall pass" attitude
Some of my favorite words in Scripture are "and it came to pass". Seasons don't come to stay, they come to pass. Isn't that so glorious?

As you walk through the season, you might have good days when your faith is "up there" and down days when you are wondering where God is and when the desert season will end. Don't dwell on your seemingly erratic faith and allow it to pull you down. Don't slip into "if only I had enough faith, maybe we'd be at a better place" spectacle.

In Luke 17, the disciples asked Jesus to increase their faith. Jesus told them "If you have faith as small as a mustard seed, you can say to this mulberry tree, 'Be uprooted and planted in the sea,' and it will obey you."

The power of faith is not tied to the amount of faith you have, but the Person you have faith in. In other words, faith in an all-powerful God is what makes the difference.

On those dry days, keep moving forward; don't camp. Don't beat yourself up for not feeling a certain way, or get upset with your husband when he doesn't sound spiritual or faith-filled. Absolutely encourage one another in faith. But keep in mind that Christ is intimately acquainted with your sorrows; He knows where you are.

I love that Christ says it's the sick - discouraged, struggling, disheartened folk - that need a doctor. Not the healthy happy, whole folks. So certainly He won't toss you out when you are overwhelmed; He will carry you and strengthen you.

7. Accept help if it's there but don't sacrifice your marriage for it
Finally, an area where we sometimes stumble as wives.

You've been praying and trusting and it looks like God is answering prayers through some people. However, the help has a lot of strings attached. Your husband is uncomfortable. Or the other way round, your husband is okay but you are uncomfortable with all the drama that comes with it.

Granted, accepting any sort of help will feel uncomfortable. But I am talking about overzealous "helpers" who want to be in charge of the resources they are giving. People who want to instruct your life and give you grief when you don't do their bidding.

In these uncomfortable situations, Proverbs 10:22 ESV is a great guide: "The blessing of the LORD makes one rich, And He adds no sorrow with it."

If it's the Lord, it will come with peace. If people are trying to run your life, politely stand your ground, even if it means handing back their help. Don't sacrifice your marriage for help. Don't allow your needs to drive a wedge between you and your husband, between you and God.

Keep your hope in God, not man.

Winding Up

No matter what season you find yourself - in plenty or in need – always keep your eyes on God. Seasons come and go but God is constant.

Encourage financial conversations in your marriage but be kind and sensitive. Your husband might not be overjoyed to talk about money but your sensitivity and wisdom can win him over. Remember that money-talks zero in on him as a provider and put the spotlight on his habits and perspective. For those times when you can't find agreement and there are repercussions ahead, involve a trusted third party.

Keeping the spark alive

"Success is neither magical nor mysterious. Success is the natural consequence of consistently applying the basic fundamentals."

Jim Rohn

Before a job interview, most interviewees will study for the position they are interviewing for. Rarely, except maybe for the naive and inexperienced, will someone walk into an interview room without any sort of prior preparation.

However, once they land the job, the real work begins! It's no longer a matter of impressing a panel of interviewers but about performance and results.

But what does it take to produce those results that ensure they retain their job? Some sweat, owning the company's visions and mission, more study and growth.

In the same way, most people will study and prepare hard for relationship. He works hard to woo you; you work hard to be attractive and likable. All the way to your wedding.

And then you slacken.

But the work can't stop after you say "I do.". You have to put in effort into developing your marriage!

And not just any kind of effort, say, after giving your best to your career or school or kids or ministry. Marriage cannot thrive on leftover attention. It has to be the best attention.

Proverbs 12:24 says, "The hand of the diligent will rule, But the lazy man will be put to forced labor."

You have to be diligent and focused in order to move from the blues to the bliss of a grounded marriage.

Ronald Reagan said "The man (or woman) who puts into the marriage only half of what he owns will get that out."

So as we finish up this book, I want to leave you with some ideas on how to prioritize your marriage in order to harvest the good you desire.

Because without intentional investment, your marriage will turn its wheels in Blues-land, even as Bliss-ville sparkles within your reach.

Polish Your Treasure

Throughout the book we have looked at the early marriage years "hot spots" and I've offered practical ideas and tips on how to navigate them.

But make no mistake, marriage soars, not when we fixate on the challenges (though solving challenges is paramount) but when we focus on fanning the good and positive.

When you focus on polishing your treasure, intentionally investing in your marriage as opposed to putting out the fires, you find yourselves walking on the slippery roads less often. And when you face those challenging times, your connection and investment helps you find solutions faster.

So here are some areas to be proactive about in the early years of marriage:

1. Be givers
Many of us appreciate the importance of having mentors pour into us but often fail to understand the importance of pouring out to others. Receiving without giving leaves us stale and stagnant, but pouring out energizes the relationship.

When it comes to understanding and retaining principles, teaching them to others helps cement them to your memory.

So whether you are one day married or seven years married, you have something to share with others. As a newlywed, you can encourage others who are just navigating courtship or other newlyweds. An older-wed can impact courting couples, newlyweds and those within or slightly above their years.

In 1 Timothy 4:12 NLT, Paul, advises Timothy with these words: "Don't let anyone think less of you because you are young. Be an example to all believers in what you say, in the way you live, in your love, your faith, and your purity."

The weight here was on Timothy and what he thought about himself. Paul told him "don't let anyone think less of you. Focus on this..."

In the same way, it's what you think about yourself that matters the most. Don't disqualify yourself and don't allow others to disqualify you because of your seemingly limited knowledge and experience in marriage. *You know something*. Focus on sharing what you know and watch God pour through you.

In case you didn't know, many newlyweds or soon-to-be weds are drawn to new couples like a magnet because they are so fresh and passionate! You relate much better, you feel each other's pains, laugh over the same crazy findings and enjoy the same type of fun. So don't disqualify yourselves, thinking that you have nothing to give. Instead, look for opportunities to encourage and bless others. Befriend courting couples, invite them to your house, hang out with them after church, offer to buy them coffee. Go out of your way to be a blessing and watch what your giving does to your own marriage!

2. Don't neglect your mentors.
I am assuming courtship wasn't a solo experience. I hope you looked for and found a mentor couple to walk with you. After the wedding, don't do what many couples do; "release" themselves from mentorship.

Look at it this way: When a baby is born, the mother does not wash her hands off the baby because her job of carrying a baby is done. On the contrary, her work has only begun. She rolls up her sleeves and begins to work - feed, clean, change dirty diapers, love and nurture.

As you settle down in marriage, don't cut off your mentors. Let them know that you want to continue drawing and learning from them. Obviously, your relationship will change after the wedding. But don't go off by yourselves thinking you'll never need anyone any more. Instead, continue to hang out with them, invite them to your house, have coffees and meals together. The great thing about maintaining this kind of relationship is that it then becomes easier to open up about any challenges you might experience.

3. Keep growing as a person.
Your personal growth and development is important to your marriage. Actually, your happily-ever-after depends on it!

When you stagnate as a person, the whole unit (husband + wife) suffers. Stagnation comes when we forget who we are and what God has called us to do with our lives; when we fixate on one area at the expense of another (e.g. relaxation over work), when we start to "settle" down in marriage and forget to stoke our God-given dreams.

It's important to remember that God brought you together for a reason; to glorify Him. But when one or both of you neglect your potential, skills and gifts, that does not glorify God.

Marriage, ideally, should be an incubator of greatness where world changers are nurtured and unleashed into the world.

Ecclesiastes 4:9 KJV says "Two are better than one, because they have a good reward for their labor."

There are goals I had as a single girl that went unfulfilled till I got married. I longed to quit my job and dive into the passions of my heart but I was never able to. But three months to my wedding, I was able to quit my somewhat-cushy managerial job and start the interesting road of purpose pursuit.

It turned out pursuing one's purpose is not an easy cut-and-dry process. I have needed all the help God blessed me with in form of my husband. I have leaned on him for support and strength as I pursue my dreams of writing, capacity building and entrepreneurship. He's put food on the table, paid the bills, taken care of us as I worked, often without significant source of income. He's encouraged me when I wanted to quit (just today he carried me, literally, into the office and sat me on my chair to work on this book), he pays for all the expenses associated with offering free services like my blog www.IntentionalToday.com (the "free help" costs!). With my husband on my side, I have been able to do things for which I had no mental, emotional or financial capacity to do before.

It's not just one sided. My husband confesses he stayed longer in a previous job because I brought a "stability and patience factor" into his life.

Your marriage ought to push you into your next level as an individual. Physically, it's possible to see that manifest in form of a child, if God blesses you with one. But it should not stop there. There has to be a new mental, relational, social, financial fruit in your lives too!

The Drifting Problem

No one needs to tell you that life gets busy after the wedding. If you are waiting for opportunities of growth and success to fall on you, without any intentional effort on your part, you are going to wait for a very long time. Because there'll always be something else you could do besides stretch yourself and reach for your dream.

Renowned author and personal development leader, the late Jim Rohn said "The problem with drifting is that you cannot drift your way to the top of a mountain."

That's our biggest challenge as early-weds; the "drift" mindset. We have great dreams and desires for our marriage and lives but underestimate or completely ignore the kind of effort it takes to achieve them.

But growth, whether personal or as a couple, comes at a price. And so you must be ready to push beyond personal comfort zones. God might ask you to do something wild, like move countries (okay, that's my husband and I!). Or He might ask you to babysit a neighbor's child.

Maybe your growth will come in the form of going back to school to build a certain skill which is in line with your passion/calling (I am not a big fan of going back to school for going-back-to-school sake. I believe school must mean something!). As a couple you'll be called to support one another, to cheer and encourage one another in such seasons.

Right now might be a good time to begin to ask God what He wants to do with your life. Talk out your dreams with your beloved. Harmonize those aspirations and goals you had before marriage, make your vision one and plain (Habakkuk 2:2).

We like to talk about "settling down" in marriage. But a thriving happily-ever-after never settles in that sense; it's always active, never passive!

4. Slow down and engage your minds

My business mentor says that people like to think they are thinking while in reality, they are not. I can still hear him thundering from the front of the class "Think (about) what you are thinking!"

To process your thought life, he advocates to take time alone with a pen, paper or journal and write down specific thoughts concerning different areas of life. Areas that need clarity, places you need to make clear decisions, areas you are seeking God for answers.

Set time aside in your busy married life, to think critically. Don't allow any old thought to fly through your mind without direction or order. Instead capture the thoughts, sort them out and align them with the word of God.

As a wife, you'll quickly discover that your man needs time to think. *Alone.*

I like to spend all my waking hours with my husband, so I know how "giving him space" feels like; *it doesn't always feel good.* I am the type that feels sad when he has to leave for work and I count the hours till he's back home. When he's home I want to hog all his time! But over time I have learned to drag myself from his side when he needs some alone time.

"Thinking time" is not just important for your husband, it's important for you too. Sometimes the reason you are so flustered, frustrated, disappointed, bordering on exhaustion is because you haven't taken time to slow down and think through your lives critically; identifying priorities, re-aligning your life to those priorities, making adjustments and changes and cutting out things that drain you.

5. Cultivate honeymoon habits

Honeymoon years are indeed wonderful, once you learn how to navigate and overcome newlywed challenges. I encourage you to maximize this time when it's just the two of you, to discover and cultivate habits you enjoy as a couple.

It doesn't have to be extraordinary things - just something you both enjoy. My husband and I love to get into the car and discover new places. We love sunsets. We love to retreat to these things after particularly busy weeks. (Or long dreary winters.)

Practice these now, when you have the time and margin. And when life gets busier - with children, careers, business - you can retreat to these activities to reconnect.

Sow good seeds now and you will reap a bumper harvest later.

6. Keep making deposits.

In his book *Making Love Last Forever*, Dr Gary Smalley talks about "good marital banking."

He describes "a deposit as anything positive, security-producing - anything that gives your mate energy. It's a gentle touch, a listening ear, a verbalized "I love you", a fun shared experience. etc. A withdrawal is anything sad or negative - anything that drains energy from your mate. It's a harsh word, an unkempt promise, being ignored, being hurt, being controlled."[1]

Some "deposits" are easier to make than others; buying a gift for her or fixing him a good meal for example, that's easy. But fanning your love for years on end will take intentional sustained effort.

Darlene Schacht, Author and founder of The Time Warp Wife community points out "Long-lasting love doesn't happen by accident. We don't find ourselves holding hands after twenty-five years with the one that we love by pure chance. Love is deliberate, it's intentional, it's purposeful, and in the end it's worth every minute that we give of ourselves to another."[2]

It's in the Details

As you think about making deposits into your spouse's love tank, think about the things that made you fall in love with each other.

For the husbands reading this book, if she loved flowers and fruits when you were pursing her, I assure you she still wants them now. And not just fruits plopped into her kitchen sink right from the market. But the sweet wrapped bouquet and basket, presented the same way it was presented during courtship.

And for you wife, if your husband loved sports and you tagged along, nay shouted the loudest, during tournaments when you were courting, he hopes to see you cheering from the benches after marriage.

We change after marriage; no one remains the same forever, so become a student of your spouse. What speaks love today might not speak love tomorrow. She might like flowers today, but after the kids, she might value you spending time with the kids. Your husband might like your entrepreneurial wisdom and insights, but when his business is struggling, he might need your comfort and encouragement more than your gutsiness.

Stay in that student's seat. Keep learning and never stop serving your spouse.

7. Don't chase perfection

Many single ladies are appalled by single guys who search for Proverbs 31 wife in single women. To refresh your memory, Proverbs 31 describes the virtuous wife. This lady knows how to take care of herself, her man, her home, her children, her workers, her business, without breaking a sweat. Seemingly.

The problem here though, and the reason single ladies are upset, is because they cannot meet the high "Proverbs 31 Wife" standards, for the simple reason that they are not married yet. A single woman can have the *potential* of a Proverbs 31 wife, but she cannot embody all those characteristics because she is not married. You can't learn wifehood until you become a wife.

Such dilemmas and angsts are not confined to singlehood - they follow us into marriage. Immediately after marriage, we discover that we want spouses to bag the "spouse of the year" award asap. We forget that he has never had to carry the provider/protector/leadership mantle before. He did say "I do" and gave you a ring but the action did not translate to immediate transformation. It takes time, effort and practice to become a great husband.

You might be thinking that I'm cutting your husband a lot of slack. Think about yourself. As a brand new bride, you have never submitted to a husband or juggled career and family or understood what it means to become one-flesh. You don't say "I do" and suddenly know all the ways of a wife. It takes time.

I am saying that to say this; extend grace to yourselves. Allow yourselves to learn without growing overly frustrated and intimidated by the process.

Before I got married, I was a leader in my church for many years. I loved mentoring and discipling and we had many adventures in our tight knit group. After marriage, I changed direction and my husband and I started mentoring courting couples and marrieds. After a while we started organizing couples retreats and day workshops. All within the first two years of marriage. The good side to this? You grow up very fast. There's this incredible blessing of being involved in other people's lives. Such satisfaction in pouring out your life out to the Lord. The not-so-great side? There was incredible pressure on our young marriage. The enemy loves to strike at the heart of your ministry and we faced tremendous pressure as a result. We had the usual fights and disagreements of a young couple but we were at this place in "ministry" where we needed our marriage to be healthy in order to function well.

Sadly, we did not extend much grace to ourselves. At least I did not. I was horrified by our squabbles and misunderstandings. At some point I was blaming my husband, thinking that he was "ruining our ministry". After all, I did not have relationship issues before he showed up!

But God, in His mercy, had surrounded us with two wonderful couples, who also happened to be our pastors. They kept us grounded and listened to us. I remember at some point one of them told us to slow down on the marriage conferences and focus on our marriage.

So I am telling you this so you can learn from our own growing pains; don't over extend yourselves. Accept your pace and don't be in a rush. Ask God to give you a heart that is content in Him and your marriage, no matter where you are. Don't be all bent out of shape, trying to fulfill mandates that are beyond you. If a burden is too heavy for your marriage and relationship, bow out.

Apostle Paul said "I know what it is to be in need, and I know what it is to have plenty. I have learned the secret of being content in any and every situation, whether well fed or hungry, whether living in plenty or in want. I can do everything through Him who gives me strength" Philippians 4:12-13 NIV

God will give you strength and grace, but you need to be listening and obeying every step of the way.

8. Choose to be happy

Young couples are advice magnets. They don't even need to ask for it, it shows up, unsolicited. As you cultivate your happily-ever-after, you have to choose what to accept and what to reject.

I learned, the hard way, that there is no neutral gear in marriage. You are either actively rejecting wrong advice - through engaging God's truth, or passively trying to ignore wrong advice, which, sadly, is not possible because passivity is as good as acceptance.

Deuteronomy 30:19 NLT says, "Today I have given you the choice between life and death, between blessings and curses. Now I call on heaven and earth to witness the choice you make. Oh, that you would choose life, so that you and your descendants might live!"

The choice is yours. There'll never be a shortage of "voices" in your marriage, so you might as well quit wishing everyone would leave you alone! People are free to have, even air, their opinions. But they are not free to impose it on you.

Winding Up

I have spent most of our time together detailing the less than pretty parts of the early marriage years and how to navigate them. God wanted me to write these things because He wants you to press through the less than lovely season. Wedded bliss is right in front of you, just beyond the storm.

I leave you with a story shared by author & founder of Happy Wives Club, Fawn Weaver:

"A few months after we were married, Keith and I were at a couples retreat hosted by my parents. After one of the sessions, we were riding up in the crowded elevator back to our hotel room. As usual, Keith's arms were wrapped around my shoulders and my head was buried in his chest. One of the women on the elevator ride, observing our affection, began doing what so many had done before her; "Hold on to that. It won't last long_" But before she could even finish her less than positive statement, a friend of my parents added her two cents *"Happiness is a choice.* My husband and I have been married twenty nine years and we have chosen to be happy. Every morning when we wake up, we choose to enjoy our day with each other. We choose to be happy" With that she looked at Keith and me squarely in the eyes and said "Choose to be happy together and it will last."[3]

Choose to be happy together and it will last.

Notes & References

Walk Down Memory Lane

1. "The Good News About Marriage," by Shaunti Feldhahn, looks into the U.S. Census data and survey data and finds that the Christian divorce rate is 30-50% lower than the secular divorce rate. The original study that said we had the same divorce rate was by George Barna, and he simply asked people to self-identify their religion, not about whether they actually went to church. He's gone public to say that people have misused his survey data. When you actually measure things like whether people pray or go to church, the divorce rate drops significantly, closer to 15%." - Author & Speaker Sheila Wray Gregoire on http://tolovehonorandvacuum.com/2014/09/real-divorce-rate/

Chapter 1
1. http://www.amazon.com/When-Sinners-Say-Do-Discovering/dp/0976758261
2. "Take By Force: Faith that Stands Firm in the Face of Opposition" Judy Jacobs, Chapter 3
3. http://www.gotquestions.org/agape-love.html#ixzz3EpPszD2S

Chapter 2
1. http://sukofamily.org/
2. Thomas, Dr. Gary, The Five Love Languages
3. Blog post http://www.the-generous-husband.com/2014/09/30/i-was-wrong-and-a-change/
4. http://www.biblestudytools.com/pastor-resources/illustrations/misunderstood-truth-11543534.html

Chapter 3
1. http://www.readbag.com/edis-ifas-ufl-pdffiles-fy-fy04400
2. Boundaries in Marriage; Understanding The Choices That Make or Break Loving Relationships," Henry Cloud & John Townsend

Chapter 4
1. Paul Byerly, http://www.the-generous-husband.com/2013/08/16/strong-women-need-strong-men/
2. John Piper http://www.desiringgod.org/sermons/husbands-who-love-like-christ-and-the-wives-who-submit-to-them)
3. Matthew Henry's Commentary on the Whole Bible: Complete and Unabridged in One Volume
4. John Piper http://www.desiringgod.org/sermons/husbands-who-love-like-christ-and-the-wives-who-submit-to-them
5. http://scottwoodward.org/marriage_helpmeet_ezerkenegdo.html)
6. Moore, B., The Beloved Discipline, p. 319, Kindle Edition
7. Mary Kassian, on http://www.girlsgonewise.com/7-misconceptions-about-submission/

Chapter 5
1. I recommend you pick up this wonderful book by Dr. Emerson Eggerichs, "Love and Respect:

The Love She Most Desires, The Respect He Desperately Needs."
2. http://www.lifeofasteward.com/
3. http://messymarriage.com/
4. http://michaelhyatt.com/why-speaking-well-of-your-spouse-is-so-important.html
5. http://barbraveling.com/

Chapter 6

1. Mathew L Jacobson, http://matthewljacobson.com/2014/07/08/wants-far-think-sex-never-enough-good-man/
2. http://carm.org/biblical-purpose-of-sex
3. Heather Lindsey, on http://www.heatherllindsey.com/2014/08/why-we-waited-until-our-wedding-day-to.html
4. Sex on the Brain: 12 Lessons to Enhance Your Love Life, Daniel G. Amen, M.D
5. Here is a list of websites and blogs you can check out:
   • Sheila Wray Gregoire – www.tolovehonorandvacuum.com
   • J Parker - hotholyandhumorous.com
   • Beth Steffaniak – www.Messymarriage.com
   • Jennifer Smith - unveiledwife.com.
   • Lisa Jacobson - club31women.com.

   Read these "husband blogs" for insights into the workings and thinking of your husband:
   • Aaron Smith – www.husbandrevolution.com
   • Paul Byerly's – www.the-generous-husband.com
   • Matthew Jacobson www.mathewljacobson.com
   • Please note that while these websites have great biblical articles on sex and marriage, I haven't read everything they've written. But I do love most of what they have shared; that's why I recommend them to you.
6. http://hotholyhumorous.com/2013/10/what-i-wish-id-known-before-the-wedding-night/

Chapter 8

1. Making Love last forever, Dr Gary Smalley, Page 253
2. timewarpwife.com/?page_id=1111
3. Weaver, Fawn (2014), Happy wives club; one woman worldwide for the secrets of a great marriage, p. 250. Thomas Nelson

Acknowledgements

I am so grateful to the people who have helped bring this book to life.

- Jesus, my Lord and Savior without whom I am nothing.

- Tommy, my best friend. Thank you for your love and encouragement as I wrote this book. Your passion and determination remind me that I can do anything I set my heart to. Thank you for being my rock, the most awesome word nerd and a voice of excellence and depth in my life. I love you babe.

- My mentors Pastor Barnie and Grace Achoki, Pastor Johnny and Ann Umukoro, who have poured their lives into our lives and marriage. We are what we are (the good parts!) because of you. Thank you for affirming, encouraging, correcting and guiding us. Thank you for your love and belief in us. We thank God for you and could not ask for better spiritual parents and mentors.

- My mum, for showing me what true love and devotion looks like in marriage. My dad, for imparting a determination, a fierceness and devotion to God, family and the things that matter. Dad, though you are with Jesus now, your legacy lives strong. I still miss you.

- Our marriage "clinic" buddies and best friends - the TO's Team - Tom & Eunice, Tim & Kate, thank you for your friendship, for providing a safe place to work through life and issues as couples. We are better because of doing life with you guys.

- My big brother Fr. Dominic, thank you for inspiring and challenging me to never stop writing at a time when I thought my poetry and fiction were unclassy and mere ranting of a naive village girl.

- My blogging friends. Thank you for your support, comments and emails. I have grown as a writer and as a wife because of being in your great company.

- George, the most gracious editor. Thank you for making sense of my runaway sentences and weird phrases and logic. Thank you for bringing coherence and beauty to the entire manuscript. Desmond, my book designer, thank you for prompt service and excellence and ability to visualize and bring ideas to life.

- My readers, thank you for reading. It's an honor and blessing to write for you. I hope this book is a blessing to you!

CONTACT THE AUTHOR

Website www.IntentionalToday.com
Email blog@IntentionalToday.com

About the Author

Ngina Otiende is a Christian wife, writer and mentor, who blogs at IntentionalToday.com where she equips the early-wed wife with tools and resources to create an intentional happily-ever after. She has a passion for women and desires to see them overcome mindsets that hinder them from becoming all God created them to be.